PASTORAL WORK AND PERSONAL COUNSELING

Pastoral Work
and
Personal Counseling

AN INTRODUCTION TO PASTORAL CARE

Russell L. Dicks, B.D., D.D.

Revised Edition

THE MACMILLAN COMPANY

New York · 1949

TO DALE AND BILLY

two little boys
who brighten our lives in dull moments,
humble our spirits in proud moments, and
warm our hearts in tender moments;
and

TO JOANNE

a little girl
who loves and is loved by all

PREFACE

PASTORAL CARE IS AS OLD AS RELIGION. IT MEANS MINISTRY TO individuals. In its traditional sense it means shepherding of souls, or cure of souls. In all primitive tribes the medicine man, who was sometimes the tribal chief, and sometimes more powerful than the tribal chief, gave pastoral care to members of the tribe in time of personal crisis. Moses spent so much time helping people with personal problems during the wanderings of the Children of Israel in the wilderness that he had to divide the people into groups and appoint pastors to look after them. Our Lord gave from a third to a half of His time, according to the gospel record, to a personal ministry. Even St. Paul, teacher and writer that he was, gave much thought and energy to individual persons and to helping them with difficulties which they faced.

Pastoral care has carried down through the ages until now, under the impact of modern psychiatry, there is a tremendous interest in this subject. In the modern period, with its mechanical and technological achievements, with its intellectual sophistication, people came to feel quite self-sufficient. Then came further developments: speed, wealth, individualism, world wars, depressions and recessions, spending, debts, and atomic energy; and individualism and self-sufficiency collapsed like a deck of cards in the wind; now people cry out for help on every side. There is no lack of willing helpers, but we find that helping people is no easy task if they are to be helped in a way that will enable them to live in a world and society which itself is in desperate need of help. Can one be helped to health in a society that is itself sick? (Sickness, by definition, meaning that which is off balance, or destructive.) It is possible for, as Dr. Karl Jung, the Zurich psychiatrist, once said, "World problems are individual problems." While it is estimated that a third of the nation's population is sick in one way or another the problem of health is an individual problem. The resources for health flow directly from the Universe to the individual person and while one's environment may interrupt the flow of those creative forces, this interruption need not be permanent. Witness the experience of our Lord upon the cross. The death which destroyed His body did not seriously affect His spirit even in the midst of suffering, because His spirit was in such complete union with the Creative Heart of the Universe. It is the task of pastoral care to assist individuals to live hopefully and creatively, for while few will be able to live as triumphantly as He did, still the same resources for health and hope, the same God He knew as Father, that supported Him and enabled Him to live as He did, are available today.

The pastor is a shepherd. A shepherd leads and directs, watches and waits, heals, rescues, supports, and protects. All of these the pastor does, not always with the same person and not with all persons, but as the need arises.

Personal counseling, or pastoral counseling, is a term which is popular these days, but it is limited in its scope and should not be used interchangeably with pastoral care, which is the all-inclusive term. Personal counseling is coming to mean pastoral care which is given in a controlled situation and in a planned, orderly way. That is, in the counselor's office by appointment. It is recognized that each conference should seldom exceed an hour in length while less than fifty minutes to an hour accomplishes little. Whether one or more conferences are held with a given person is determined by the needs of the individual and by the time that the pastor can give to a person.

Pastoral work means going to the people; in personal counseling the people come to the pastor; both are pastoral care, but neither are the whole of pastoral care. In pastoral work, often popularly but unfortunately spoken of as *visitation*, the minister goes to the hospital, the home, the place of work or business. He goes to the prison. He ministers to the physically and mentally ill, the bereaved, the aged, the shut-in, the youth, the maritally unhappy, the discouraged and fearful. He goes to the homes of his people whether they are in trouble or not, and he seeks to have them come to him. He is interested in those who are in trouble and he is interested in helping them to avoid trouble.

It is the purpose of this book to describe the field of pastoral care and the methods with which the minister works in carrying out this phase of his task. It does not seek to be definitive but only introductory. Its purpose is to give a comprehension *of* the task and to build up an enthusiasm *for* the task. While it may sharpen your understanding, it cannot teach you the mastery of pastoral care technique. That can be learned only through working at the job, and one should work first under the supervision of an experienced practitioner of the art of pastoral care. Dr. Henry von Witzleben, a psychoanalyst of Chicago, who is much interested in the field of pastoral care has said, "In the near future the minister who carries on pastoral work without special training for it may be guilty of malpractice."

Special training for pastoral work is now available in several seminaries and allied institutions; these are not all of equal merit. It is not enough to wander through a hospital, or to work as an orderly, or to read a few books. One must spend months and sometimes years in lectures and under the tutorage and discipline of a recognized pastor of ability to understand the nature of human personality and to master the delicate art of pastoral care.

Some of this material has appeared in the magazines *Pulpit Digest, New Century Leader* and *The Pastor*. I wish to express my gratitude to the editors of these magazines for permission to use the material here. Also my extreme gratitude to Miss Bernice Breede, my secretary, for her patience in preparing the manuscript and her ability in transcribing a script that even I could not read at times.

RUSSELL L. DICKS

CONTENTS

PART ONE

CONDITIONS OF EFFECTIVE PASTORAL WORK AND COUNSELING

I

THE NEW PASTORAL CARE

IN THE LAST HUNDRED YEARS MAN HAS MADE MORE PROGRESS in the conquest of pain than in all the rest of human history. Since 1900 the average life has been lengthened by twenty years. Within the next ten to fifteen years it is expected that most of the major disease-killers will be brought under control; the conquest of tuberculosis, cancer, infantile paralysis, and syphilis are upon the horizon. Heart disease—the major killer —which is a disease brought on largely by excitement—will still remain. Man's ingenuity in his struggle against pain is surpassed only by his ingenuity in creating instruments of destruction.

On the other hand we see the steady increase of nervous and mental diseases—one out of twelve of our young men was turned back at point of induction or during the early part of their training during World War II, being judged as *emotionally* unfit for military training, one out of three marriages ends in divorce, excessive drinking is rapidly increasing, well over fifty per cent of all people who go to the doctor have no organic disease and many of those who have organic conditions are suffering from diseases brought on by emotional problems.

Can modern man survive the society he has created? The answer is obvious: some can and some cannot. Every day we see people go down, some to rise up stronger for the experience of failure; some never to rise at all, or if to rise, soon to fall again. Is human behavior getting better or worse? It is getting both better and worse. Can human behavior be changed? Some of it can be assisted in its development and influenced in its growth; some cannot. Life can be made worthwhile and given meaning for some, for some little purpose can be found.

Those observers of our generation who have been most outspoken in claiming that personality cannot be changed—that it is determined by its heredity and limited by its environment—namely, the psychoanalysts and psychiatrists, have been most active in trying to influence it. A recent psychoanalytic writer has put it, "Heredity determines the upper limits of abilities and when they are normally going to increase or decrease. For example, it determines whether a man could possibly be a great musician or mathematician. . . . Environment, however, determines what he actually does. In other words, heredity determines possibilities and environment determines how closely they can be approached." [1] All of which leaves the pastor about where he was before the coming of modern psychology: with a job to do in helping people to live creatively.

Pastoral work and personal counseling deals with human beings as individuals. It works from a biased point of view. It admits quite frankly that it attempts to influence human behavior and to direct human personality in a way that it believes to be desirable, which is not to say that the pastor need be a spiritual dictator. The psychiatrist has often quarreled with us because we do work from a bias; his quarrel is not so much with our bias as with the way we use the bias in our work. We have talked about spiritual freedom, but we have been unwilling to permit people to disagree with us; we have talked about love, but we have been unable to love those who needed affection.

The psychiatrist has claimed that he works from a neutral position. There is no such position. The psychiatrist wants certain things for his patient, for instance, health; that is a bias. He maintains that he is not interested in the morals of his patient, but then we find that morals, probably more than any other single factor, affect both physical and mental health. The

[1] Berne: *The Mind in Action*, Simon and Schuster, 1947.

great lesson we have to learn from the psychiatrist at this point, however, is one that the pastor should have taught the psychiatrist, rather than having to have the psychiatrist teach to him: the simple lesson of *judge not*, but *love one another*. In our pastoral relationships we have been prone to judge rather than to understand; to criticize rather than to forgive; to dictate rather than to listen; to hurry rather than to wait; to answer rather than to question; to become apprehensive ourselves rather than to assist our parishioners to find faith; to be pessimistic rather than to be hopeful. Adolph Meyer once said, "The physician pits his health against the illness of the patient. Sometimes the patient wins." So the pastor pits his hopefulness, his confidence, his deep belief in the creativeness and purposefulness of life against the lack of hope, lack of confidence, and disbelief which he finds in the parishioner-patient.

The past two decades have seen the steady decline of pastoral work and the encroachment upon the pastoral field by other professions, particularly the medical and social work professions. The doctor has always given some—and at times a great deal of—attention to the emotional-spiritual needs of his patients. Under the leadership of modern psychiatry, which made its great advances between the first two world wars, the medical profession gives more and more attention to the emotional side of the patient, and not infrequently even attempts to deal with his spiritual needs.

Social work, the newest of all the humanitarian professions, came into being because of unmet physical needs: that is, the need for food, shelter and clothing. Social work, at its outset, was as paternalistic as the orthodox church. Gradually this point of view has shifted, under the influence of psychiatry also, until now social work is pushing steadily into the field of emotional-spiritual problems.

The clergyman's relationship with these two professions will be discussed later, but I mention them here in connection with a discussion of the decline of pastoral work simply to point out that during the time that the minister was giving less and less attention to the care of souls, other professions were giving more and more. Actually the medical and social work professions are allies, not competitors, of the minister. The church and the clergy need what they have to contribute; they also need what we have to contribute, and they need it desperately!

The major reason for the decline of pastoral work, I believe, was the change in world-outlook of the average person, both layman and clergyman. This change came about so gradually and so subtly that we were hardly conscious of it. While it was taking place our formal theology which was taught in the church changed but little, except that more and more of it was sloughed off, treated with indifference, and generally ignored. We moved into an automobile age, then an airplane age, and now into an atomic age, but we clung to a horse-and-buggy theology.

Protestant thinking of the days of the great evangelists— and the results of their work are still generally felt—was characterized by a concern about hell and salvation, but the hell was more real than the salvation. Hell has always been more real as an idea than heaven because we are more familiar with suffering, while heaven is thought of as a free gift. As practical people we are suspicious of free gifts, for we have often found a hidden clause which cancels whatever is free that we had been promised. Further, the history of mankind has been a struggle against suffering and the threat of suffering. We are able to live heroically under suffering but when free from it we go crazy with delight, for we are like children who have been given unlimited power. The result is that we have been forced to live by a negative theology—a theology loaded with suspicion, fear, and pessimism. Despite the message of love which runs through the New Testament we were never able to imagine a heavenly chorus without discords. We have been good, when we have, not because we were attracted to the good, but because we were afraid of the results of being bad.

And then the scholars loosed the information that led to the fundamentalist-liberal struggle, which is even now still rumbling around in the background of our thinking like a thunderstorm receding into the distance. Whatever else may be said of Protestant religious thinking of the early twentieth century, its chief characteristic was confusion.

This confusion was reflected in the pastoral work of the time. During the past fifteen years more has been published in any one year upon the subject of pastoral care than in the whole fifty preceding years. The fundamentalist-liberal fight of the twenties contributed both to the confusion and to the loss of authority of the clergyman in the care of souls. Even today the fundamentalist clergyman is characterized by a misuse of authority in his pastoral work while the liberal is characterized by a lack of authority. These attitudes are reflected in the kind of pastoral work each does. Both do damage and both fail to meet spiritual needs.

While the clergy were struggling over the question of how they were going to interpret the scriptures, the layman, particularly those who now are in their fifties, and whose sons and daughters accept and take for granted all kinds of scientific discoveries, lost both his belief in heaven and hell. The fifty-year-old layman, particularly if he came out of a religiously conservative background, is apt to be startled if you tell him he does not believe in hell. He is just a little frightened by the thought, for his mother believed in hell and if he admits he does not, he thinks in some mysterious way he is being unfaithful to her and therein he may lose her. Women, not being tied so closely to their mothers, by and large feel rather indifferent on the subject, depending a great deal upon what kind of marriages they have made.

The loss of the old-fashioned heaven does not bother either men or women so much. They never had a very clear picture of it anyway so they do not mind giving it up. The idea was like that of inheriting a million dollars. It could happen; one heard of those to whom it had happened, but it is not apt to happen to oneself.

While if you point out to young people, either in their twenties or thirties, that they do not believe in an old-fashioned hell and heaven they will look at you seriously for a moment and then agree without guilt feeling, "No, I guess I don't. I hadn't thought much about it, but I guess you're right." The very fact that they had not thought about it confirms the contention that heaven and hell are ideas that do not concern the younger generation and as ideas have lost their power to influence human behavior.

With the loss of heaven and hell as realistic concepts the Protestant clergyman lost his authority as a pastor and his purposes in pastoral care became confused. He continued to carry on certain types of pastoral work, such as ministry to the bereaved and a half-hearted ministry to the sick, because the same spiritual-emotional needs were present, while large areas of Protestantism gave up almost entirely its ministry to the dying. We taught a "priesthood of all believers" which was psychologically unsound, for all believers are not emotionally and intellectually capable of being priests. Many, knowing their own shortcomings, have no such desire but prefer the ministrations of another who is willing to interpret the Desires of God to them and their desires to God—particularly in times of suffering—which is the role of the priest.

I was a long time discovering this fact, for as a typical Protestant, knowing little about religion, I believed in the teaching that no man need be priest to another and every man may make his confession directly to God. As an intellectual Protestant I still believe that, but as a clinical observer I know that it is neither possible nor desirable. Some know more about life than others, and some understand more about the Mind of God than others; some have better judgment than others, and some have more faith and hope and love than others, and above all, some stand freer from suffering than others. When we are sick we go to a physician because he understands illness and knows how to help us, but none of us would be satisfied to be treated by a doctor who himself was acutely ill at the time we sought treatment.

When suffering closes down upon us we want someone to help us spiritually, as we want someone to help us physically, who stands free from acute suffering himself; who knows and cares about our needs, but whose faith is strong and whose courage is high. The old heaven and hell have passed away and the old-fashioned authority of the clergyman with them, but the same spiritual-emotional needs remain, and out of those needs arises a new authority. This authority comes to one not because he has been set aside by an ordination ceremony, but because of one's understanding and affection, and through one's use of those forces. In that sense authority may come to any believer, making him a priest who seeks to help his fellow creature.

Some may think that this is humanism. It is not. It is founded upon a belief that God is within us, around us, beyond us; that He is creative, maintaining order in some areas and seeking to establish order in others. As human beings, we may become heirs and co-heirs, creators and co-creators with Him. As a minister I am interested in helping people to become creative, so is the doctor, and the nurse, and the social worker, and the teacher, for all of these belong to the humanitarian professions. If one is a carpenter his creativity takes another form, if a street-car conductor, still another, if a housekeeper, still another.

There are many who, due to various reasons, most of which are beyond our control, fail to develop creative capacities, while others develop them only slightly. To participate in the creative role, to share with God in carrying responsibility is to have gained the kingdom of heaven already—perhaps one should say, released the kingdom of heaven within us—while to fail to accept such responsibility, or to fail to develop one's capacities to enable one to accept *creative responsibility*, is to accept hell.

A parent who pampers a child, over-protecting him, and tying him closely to her, is condemning him to hell. To be sure her own emotional limitations in turn may have their roots in her mother's emotional problems. In other words our going to hell is delayed by a generation, but the ultimate results are about the same as they were under an old-fashioned theology.

Some may think that this rules out a conception of Christ as Mediator and as a Member of the Trinity. It does not. As I said before, we do not know to what extent we are responsible for developing our creative capacities. The life of Christ and His influence in history contribute directly to the kind of lives we live: through the culture we are born into, the homes that nurture us, the schools we attend, the hospitals that serve us, the ideals we live by, and the love that flows through us. Christ is a Mediator, both in history and in the contemporary scene, but He is not a Complete Mediator in that we have no responsibility for our destinies or for those of our children. There is one further thought in this connection that influences our pastoral work: the nature of Christ's death is of relatively little importance so far as the pastor's work is concerned. That is, it was not necessary for Jesus to have been murdered by religious zealots and mercenary soldiers for me as a pastor to be helpful to a girl who has become pregnant out of wedlock, and who is upon the point of committing suicide because of guilt feelings. However, the fact that Christ lived and taught and died the *kind of death* He did may well be responsible, at least partially, for the fact that I care whether a girl commits suicide or not. Especially Christ may be responsible for the kind of understanding and hope and compassion I bring to such a person.

The question is often raised as to how much psychiatry has influenced the thought of the clinically trained clergyman and wherein our theology has shifted. Obviously it has influenced us greatly, we think for the better. It has caused us to sharpen our thinking; to become more disciplined and less sentimental and it has made us critical of easy answers, for easy answers to deep spiritual problems do more harm than good. While we have been appreciative of the teachings of psychiatry concerning the nature of human personality we have often found ourselves critical of its short-range goals concerning human behavior. We are not content with adjusting a sick person to a sick environment. Increasingly psychiatry is recognizing this fact also.

We have to admit, however, that psychiatry, and to a lesser degree, social work, are largely responsible for the rise of what I would call *the new pastoral care*. At the same time we would claim that clinical training, as developed by the Reverend Anton Boisen at Worcester, Massachusetts, and William Kellar, M.D., at Cincinnati, Ohio, has made most of whatever significant contribution there has been from theological circles to this field, the work of Carl Stolz of Hartford, Connecticut, and Charles Holman of Chicago, Illinois, notwithstanding. Both Stolz and Holman were interpreters of the new psychology for pastors, drawing heavily from psychiatry, but neither made any particular original contribution themselves in their early writings. The work of the Reverend Elwood Worcester and the Reverend Samuel McComb and their Immanuel Movement in Boston preceded both the new psychology and Cabot-Boisen clinical training.[2]

The Immanuel Movement which had its start at the Imman-

2 Cabot and Boisen were co-founders of clinical training for the clergy, for Richard Cabot, M.D., originally made the plea for "a clinical year for theological students" and later used both his influence and his checkbook in helping Dr. Boisen start such work at the Worcester State Hospital in 1925. He did the same thing for me at the Massachusetts General Hospital in Boston in 1933. While still later he endowed the work there, which is now carried on through the Institute of Pastoral Care, founded by the Reverend Rollin J. Fairbanks. The Council for Clinical Training, Inc., which was originally incorporated in Massachusetts in 1930 and later shifted to New York, and which was the original parent organization, still continues its work with offices at 2 East 103rd Street, New York City. The Reverend Philip Guiles, one of Dr. Boisen's early students, established his own work independently of the Council for Clinical Training in 1933, and is now professor of pastoral psychology at Andover-Newton Theological School, Newton Centre, Massachusetts. Dr. William Keller's School of Applied Religion, which was started

uel Church (Episcopal) in Boston while Elwood Worcester was rector there, was a religion and health movement which was active during the late teens and twenties. It failed because Elwood Worcester insisted that those who came to him for help must give up their own physicians and go to doctors who were active in his movement.

Clinical training has consistently plugged away at investigating and describing the pastoral task since its inception in 1925. There have been marked differences of opinion among the leaders of the Cabot-Boisen tradition, some of which have turned upon differences concerning ideas and some upon clashes of personality. Henry Sloane Coffin, then President of Union Theological Seminary in New York City, used to say, "The personal adjustment people can't adjust." Perhaps it was well we could not, for we fought hard for what we believed, forcing each other to clarify and present our views.

The Cabot-Boisen followers would agree that experience for clergy must meet three qualifications to be classed as clinical training: (1) the student must work with people, (2) he must keep records of his work, (3) and he must do his work under qualified supervision. Where he does his work is of relative unimportance, although this point has caused much bloodshed among us in the past and is still believed to be of great importance by some. The student may learn much from books and articles but we are not satisfied until he studies *the living record*: the human being.[3]

While psychiatry and the new psychology cracked the subject open, we believe clinical training is responsible for reclaiming the pastoral task for the contemporary minister and for the rise of *the new pastoral care*. We would be the first to

---

in 1925 also, is now affiliated with the Episcopal Theological School in Cambridge, Massachusetts, and continues its tradition in the person of the Reverend Joseph A. Fletcher.

[3] See Appendix A.

say that the task is only well begun and that there is more that we do not know than we do know, but we have begun and are now well established.

The clergyman's task in pastoral work is to assist spiritual forces at work within the individual; forces which are struggling for growth and maturity of the soul. These forces follow laws which are as dependable as are the laws of health within the physical body. In fact, we are recognizing that the spiritual and physical affect each other so profoundly that many observers claim they are but different parts of the same whole.

Life is a growing process, a maturing experience, a stabilizing force—never finished, never complete. The purpose of living is to develop spiritually mature human beings; maturity to the place of accepting and carrying through responsibility in the creative process of the universe of which we are a part; maturity to the place that we may feel comfortable without forcing our wills upon others; maturity to the place that we are willing to let others be free, thus gaining freedom for ourselves. We gain maturity of soul so that we may come into fellowship with God which is to gain eternity, or the immortal life.

As a parent I love my child. I cannot explain why, there are a dozen, a thousand reasons. He may tear my heart through his suffering, but as a wise parent I know he must be permitted to live his life, to find his way to school, to defend himself against the neighborhood bully. I also know he faces the possibility of *becoming* the neighborhood bully unless as a father I am wise enough to avoid bullying his mother, brother and himself. What a hard job it must be to be God!

It is the pastor's task to assist that maturing, growing, developing life in his parishioners and those who seek his help. Some will need a great deal for a little while; others will need it for a long time; some will need a little for a little while; others will need none at all. It is the pastor's task to discover the need and to attempt to meet it. Throughout his work he must be alert lest he make the mistake God does not make: he must not live someone else's life.

As clergymen we are not content with *relieving* suffering as the physician and social worker are. To be sure we are concerned that suffering shall be relieved; witness the church's building of hospitals and colleges for the care of the sick and the relief of ignorance, that the abundance of nature may be tapped for mankind; but with all this we are not content. It is not enough to be free from want and to have health. As clergymen we are concerned with what you do with health when you have it. It is the pastor's task to work to relieve suffering and fear and loneliness, but it is also his task to assist people to gain faith and hope and that fellowship with God which encompasses eternity itself. This may be accomplished even though suffering is not relieved. It is accomplished sometimes not only in spite of suffering but because of suffering. One of the most spiritually mature people I have met is a woman who has never walked a step in her life.

As we think of ourselves as God's assistants let us be certain of our point of view. There is much of mystery in religion for there is much in the Mind of God we do not understand, and this will always be true since our perspective is limited. Three times, twice in calm moments and a third in a heated moment of suffering, our Lord seemed to portray the Mind of God more clearly than at any other time. Once He told the story of a Samaritan, whom He described as "good," who picked up a stricken man beside the road. Our Lord did not speak of the spiritual care of the man upon the Jericho road, but we assume that it was implied in the story in the phrase, "he had compassion upon him." Another time our Lord clearly revealed God's Mind in His story of the Prodigal Son. The son was returning home, asking only that he be permitted to work in his father's fields. To his amazement, and to ours today whenever it happens to us, for this is one of the great mysteries of religion, *the father was out upon the road to welcome his son's return*. There was no thought in the father's mind of the son's going to the fields. The point of the story is the father's attitude toward the boy's shame.

Finally, upon the cross our Lord demonstrated the Mind of God in turning that tragic experience into one of triumph. The cross was tragic and we must never overlook that fact. There was suffering there over and above the suffering of our Lord. Mary, His mother, was there, and Mary Magdalene, who loved Him deeply, His disciples, His followers and friends, and all those who looked for a new day for the poor, dispirited and discouraged. There was tragedy in the blind prejudice of those who misunderstood Him and caused Him to be put to death. There was tragedy in the pitiable weakness of Pilate and in the blind brute-strength of the soldiers who raised the cross with Him upon it. There was tragedy in our Lord's suffering, but beyond the suffering there was the peace, the quiet strength, the hope that His mastery of the cross revealed. There we see the deeper Mind of God.

These three scenes the pastor must have burned into his soul as he sets out upon his task; the giving of physical relief to the man upon the Jericho road, the father out upon the road to welcome the returning son, and finally, the triumphant living that may come out of suffering and tragedy, even out of death itself. In the light of these revelations the pastor goes to his task with a quiet confidence that God is about His work in the universe and that they who make understanding and compassion a part of wisdom are privileged to assist Him.

II

THE PERSONAL CRISIS

IN ONE SENSE THE STUDY OF THE PERSONAL CRISIS IN AN EF-fort to understand spiritual needs is a negative approach. As clergymen and religionists we run the danger of becoming abnormally interested in people with problems. In this respect we may limit our work by becoming content with the relief of suffering and giving little attention to the prevention of suffering, as is true of most physicians. Preventive lags behind curative medicine because the latter is more interesting and dramatic. The intimate and satisfying personal relation between patient and physician is far more interesting than the emotional relationship between a man and a mosquito swamp. Fortunately there are a few who prefer the latter.

Because the person who is suffering needs what we have, we naturally are attracted to him. This is as it should be, but we must not be content to give attention only to people with problems. The person who is not suffering has affection and faith already but needs to share them with those who need help. Some refuse to carry their part of this load and it becomes the pastor's task to enlist their interest; all too often he fails in this task. Psychology will eventually teach us why.

A basic principle in pastoral work is the recognition that life is a shifting, developing, regressing, growing experience. One thing in human nature we can be certain of is that people are different from each other and that a person is different from his former self at one time as judged against another time. Different ideas, different moods, different interests, hopes, apprehensions, and loyalties claim his attention from time to time. The pastor must be capable of recognizing these various conditions and must adapt himself to them. We must start with the parishioner where *he* is, not where we are. Since so much of our lives are lived against the background of suffering, in fact since creation comes out of suffering, we must give attention to the suffering experience. The personal crisis gives the clergyman his reason and opportunity for doing pastoral work. Without suffering we would not have religion, the church, or much of life as we know it. Suffering seems to be deep in the heart of the universe.

Religion had its rise in man's effort to establish a satisfactory and satisfying relationship with the world in which he lived. In primitive religion man sought to overcome suffering and the forces which threatened to destroy him; modern man does the same. It is late in the history of religion that man is religious because he gains satisfaction through being religious, when love of God displaces fear of God. Only out of suffering is deep love born.[1]

We can observe suffering as the primary moving force behind creation. At the same time we see suffering which is destructive, which fails. We must not make the mistake of glorifying suffering, lest it become an end in and of itself, but we take courage from the fact that good may come out of it. Without that belief and without the support of that knowledge it is doubtful if many of us would long remain nurses, doctors, social workers, or pastors. We would be like unarmed children going out to battle against giants.

There are four types of suffering and, it seems, only four: pain, fear, guilt feelings, and loneliness. Some observers list apprehension, worry, resentment and anger as additional types. The difference between apprehension and fear is only one of degree, and both may stem from guilt feelings. Resentment

[1] For an excellent treatment of the whole subject of suffering see *Victorious Suffering* by Glover. Abingdon-Cokesbury Press, Nashville and New York, 1942.

and anger stem from fear. We do not feel resentment and we do not become angry until we have been hurt physically or mentally, or until we face the danger of being hurt. The emotion of fear may be different chemically from anger, but fear sets off anger. Therefore anger and fear should be studied and treated as one emotion.

These four emotions are the foundation stones of human behavior; the whole of life has to do with them. The struggle to avoid suffering accounts for our industrial, social, economic, recreational and religious life, and for our heroism in searching for new ways of life and living. To be sure, these four emotions are mixed up together, so that seldom do we deal with one apart from another, and then not for long.

A. *Pain*

Physical pain is the pure emotion; all others seem to have some relation to it in one way or another. It may be brought about by hunger, thirst, exposure, injury or disease. The severity of pain varies depending upon its cause; the pain brought about by angina pectoris is reported to be one of the most severe, while a person may have a leg severed and feel little pain at the time.

Pain has its positive values: without it we would not stir ourselves to work to secure the basic necessities of life, nor would we have developed powers of observing, and harnessing the productivity of nature; without pain we should fall prey to the various kinds of injury and disease without seeking medical care. Pain is basic and primitive in our natures; we hold it in common with other creatures of the animal kingdom.

Our lives are made up of little pains and we take them in our stride as the child learning to walk takes bumps and tumbles but gets up and tries again. But prolonged physical suffering we do not handle so well. Intellectually, emotionally and spiritually we lose our perspective; our confidence in our world goes to pieces. Our reasoning powers are the first to break under the pressure of prolonged suffering, but we have the power of observation which leads us to search for the cause of suffering even in the midst of it and for ways of gaining relief. Then we are close to the rise of primitive religion, for primitive man personalized everything around him. It will be a triumphant day when we dismiss the thought that our physical suffering is brought about by evil spirits or comes to us as punishment, but even in our seemingly enlightened age many still believe suffering is punishment. To be sure, some suffering is the result of wrong-doing but not all.

Pain needs to be listed with other emotions as a symptom for spiritual need only because we have been taught through the Hebrew and Christian religions that God will do all things for us if we pray hard enough. In that teaching there has been no recognition of time: that relief from suffering takes time, often a great deal of time, and even then the forces of nature and man may fail in gaining that relief. Further, our religious teaching has not pointed out clearly enough the positive values of pain; for unless viewed from the perspective of time and the larger experience of living, pain is destructive. It has a way of teaching many lessons when we are willing to accept them. It was ten years after a severe illness before I came to appreciate what I had learned there.

A woman I know had been in the hospital for three years; during that time she had suffered great pain for prolonged periods of time. One day she said, "Mr. Dicks, I would not have missed this experience for the world." I said, "What do you mean?" She said, "Through this experience of being ill and suffering I have found a faith. When I became ill I did not believe in prayer or know how to pray. Now I do." Her quiet endurance in the midst of her suffering verified her statement; unfortunately others, many others go through such experiences with different results. Some have faith at the outset but lose it during their suffering. In fact, I believe that most people who have an active faith and drop out of the church do so because no one steadied them during a period of personal crisis.

B. *Fear*

Fear is the second type of personal crisis we recognize in people, particularly during illness. Dr. Joseph Fort Newton has said that more people have written him over the years about fear, on the basis of his syndicated articles, than any other problem. The difference between fear, apprehension and worry is one of degree, although the bodily changes are different in that they are more pronounced in fear than in apprehension, but their cause is the same.

One type of fear is the easily recognized condition which is acute fear. This is basic and primitive. We hold this emotion in common with other creatures. It is the body's preparation for combat or for flight. As civilized creatures, we have overcome much of the need for such strong emotions but we still have the same capacity for being frightened which our forefathers had many centuries and ages ago. The result is that these feelings often get out of control and do us harm through worry.

There is the second type of fear, not so easily recognized, but which is devastating in its effect; this is apprehension, which is the kind of fear that keeps us awake nights. It is closely tied up with guilt feelings, which will be discussed presently. Further, there seems to be a close tie-up between worry and one's attitude toward death, which also would lead us to feel that worry ties up with guilt feelings. When we worry about a loved one's possible death we are afraid of loneliness and the loss of affection and companionship. Apprehension gnaws away at one's poise and faith until one breaks completely, thus seeking relief from suffering in the insensibility of a psychosis, or so-called nervous breakdown.

The opposite of fear is faith, confidence that the world at its heart can be trusted. Some persons seem never to have been afraid, others seem to be afraid of everything, while most of us are in between, afraid sometimes and of some things, not afraid at other times. Certainly it is the part of wisdom to be afraid at times. The good soldier is one who is capable of fear, otherwise he takes unnecessary risks. The story has been told of the veteran soldier walking beside the rookie as they went into combat. The rookie looked at the color of the veteran's face and said, "You're afraid?" "Yes," replied the veteran, "if you were only half as scared as I am you would run away."

We see some persons go into the operating room frightened so badly they cannot speak, others go calmly, relaxed and at ease. This latter is a condition that is hard come by and one that grows out of the practice of faith and learning to trust. As one woman put it, "It's all right whether I get well or whether I don't, it's all right!" That was no easy resignation, but a statement of faith which she had gained through long hours of prayer.

Contrast that statement with the situation of another woman who could tell you the day, hour and place where she was "saved," yet she was afraid to go home. One of these women was simply more advanced in her faith and acceptance of God than the other.

C. Guilt Feelings

Guilt feelings are closely tied up with fear; still if it were possible to remove all fear we would still have a feeling that could be identified as a *sense of failure*. Guilt feelings underlie much of living; they are potentially present in all our decisions and behavior. We seldom are definitely conscious of a "sense of the ought," still it is the background against which we live. Without this background we would not have developed the kind of human society we have and hope to have. Just as the emotions of pain and fear make the human creature one with other creatures, so the emotion of guilt—the capacity to feel sorrow for an act—sets man apart from other creatures.

There may be many more but we can identify at least two kinds, or levels, of guilt feelings; the conscious level is one, while the unconscious sense of failure is the other. The first is apt to turn upon a single act, sometimes of a superficial nature; the second may be a single act but it is the result of cumulative thought and brooding. It is the athletic player fouling an opponent on the spur of the moment but doing it in such a way as to reveal that the act had been carefully planned, so that at the moment there was little conscious thought in the act.

We should not expect stories of guilt feelings to make sense, or for a person to be reasonable when he is suffering from a sense of guilt, for these feelings are no more reasonable than are other emotions, even though they may be understood by the sufferer.

A busy psychoanalyst spoke of treating a patient free. A friend expressed surprise, saying she did not know that he ever took anyone on a free basis. He said, "If you asked me to take someone free I would not do it, but I always have one or two such patients just to relieve my own guilt feelings." That from a psychoanalyst!

Many of the altruistic things we do probably are motivated by guilt feelings while others are done because of fear. We do not know how much the fear of death is based upon guilt feelings and how much a fear of the unknown. The minister sees a person once in a while who clearly expresses his concern about death because of guilt feelings, but not often.[2]

Guilt feelings and religion are tied up together, for it is the function of the church to describe goals of living, to hold up the ideal. The church constantly emphasizes the "ought," the way life may be lived but seldom is; organized religion works to maintain tensions within us lest we become possessed with comfort, and indifferent to the needs of others.

[2] See chapter VI.

As individuals we may go through experiences of crisis and suffering quite apart from the nation's sufferings, so that the church's practice should not be determined by the nation's condition, although its predominant message may well be. As individuals we experience this sense of failure on many occasions and we naturally look to the church for help.

If suffering of guilt feelings is prolonged without relief then people turn away from the church. The free churches, particularly, have not been realistic or helpful in their dealing with guilt feelings. They have not given their people the opportunity to express these feelings and receive reassurance that they may take up their lives again, which the liturgical churches do through the practice of confession. If confession is consistently practised the sense of guilt is not apt to become so deep-rooted and is therefore more easily relieved; also the individual communicant knows he can receive help through the church and is therefore more healthy-minded, for he knows where to turn for help.

This is not to suggest that our only concern with guilt should be to relieve it, although that seems to be the attitude of some psychiatrists and social workers who claim a sense of guilt only makes a person sick; such an attitude represents a superficial knowledge of living. How long would government hold together without a sense of responsibility? Not long. In fact democracy today faces a serious threat because more people capable of this sense of responsibility, with its corresponding capacity for feeling a sense of guilt, do not go into government work while the more basic indifference rests back upon the voters themselves and their failure to exercise the franchise. The same thing can be said about other phases of our life and living.

Guilt feelings may lead to action; but unless that action is wisely chosen then tragedy is the result. It is the function of the clergyman to direct the actions which are motivated by guilt feelings. Many clergy fail in this task because they do not know what they are dealing with; others fail because of their own biases, prejudices and suppressed guilt feelings.

Gradually the physician's consultation has been substituted for the ancient rite of confession and from that have come other substitutions until now the medical profession is increasingly taking over the care of the total person. Today the clergy is facing expulsion from the very task that brought it into existence: the care of souls. However, there are signs which indicate that the clergyman may reclaim his rightful role in this respect, but he needs the doctor and social worker as allies.

D. *Loneliness*

Loneliness underlies more human behavior than any other emotion unless it is hunger. It is not as primitive as fear and therefore not as basic but in our generation it is far more general. Loneliness permeates the whole of life; it stimulates the child's love for its parents, it is the prime emotion behind courtship, it leads to the establishing of homes and communities, for it is the background to love; it is the problem of the aged and it is the problem of bereavement. Loneliness causes us to seek new experience, to turn to adventure, to bow in worship. When in the clasp of loneliness we may become depressed or we may become aggressive.

Loneliness underlies some rather peculiar behavior. I was told of a college girl whose clothes were untidy, whose hair was never fixed, and who always needed a bath. The psychologist would explain such a person's actions or her failure to care for her person on the basis of attitudes she held toward her family, where there was little affection. She built up an attitude of "Nobody loves me; I'm an ugly duckling." It was not surprising that she was failing in school, that she had no dates, that she had no friends. Her basic problem was *loneliness*.

There are at least two kinds of loneliness that we can identify. There is a superficial, nagging, gnawing kind such as homesickness, such as the lover desiring to be with the loved one. While this is a disturbing feeling and may lead one to dire actions and desperate behavior in extreme instances, by and large it is handled fairly well by most persons. It is a condition which we recognize is temporary and nothing that a little pluck and endurance will not handle. If prolonged over a period of time without relief it may lead to serious mental depressions in some; in others it is apt to seek relief through aggressive acts such as drinking and fighting. In some girls it leads to depression, to worry, to anxiety, to sickness; in others it leads to aggressive acts toward men, to drinking, to sexual laxness.

There is a second type of loneliness which is more basic in nature and more difficult to identify. It is the kind the girl, described above, illustrates, and it rests back upon earlier experiences in the home. It is usually on a subconscious level so that the person himself does not know what causes him to act as he does. Psychologists believe it is this feeling that causes body odor, bad breath and other forms of repulsive conditions to develop within and about a person. In one girl, with whom I counseled about her pending divorce which she ultimately secured, lack of affection between her mother and father had caused her to make an early, unfortunate marriage. She married to get away from her home where there was always quarreling and because her parents gave her little affection, for they did not have it to give. She married the first man who proposed to her, and from her description of him, despite her efforts to the contrary, he seemed to be a rather desirable fellow. Once married and away from her mother and father, she found it impossible to feel real affection for her husband because she would not let herself love or be loved. She did not know how. She had two babies but felt little affection for them. At heart she is a lonely person and it is doubtful if she will ever be anything else. Religion attracted her early in life and, while she gained much from it, it tended to increase her loneliness rather than relieve it because religion is based upon faith, trust, love.

These she did not know. While she was an attractive girl she went to great pains to make herself unattractive by the way she did her hair and the way she wore her clothes. Curiously enough, she was not bitter and her personality was rather pleasant.

This deep loneliness is baffling and we have little effective treatment for it. This is the kind of frustration and restlessness that has turned out explorers and adventurers, searchers, wanderers and geniuses. The great saints and the great sinners both have been sired by this kind of loneliness.

III

THE INTERPERSONAL RELATIONSHIP

THE RELATIONSHIP, FORMERLY CALLED RAPPORT, IS THE EMO-
tional force which comes into operation when two people meet.
A similar force is present when more than two people are in
contact with each other, such as a minister and a congregation,
a teacher and a class, but since our subject is pastoral care and
since the ideal number in a pastoral contact is two—the parishioner and the pastor—I will discuss the *interpersonal relationship* only in this connection.

The relationship may be positive or negative. This is the reason that the term rapport is dropping out of use: by definition it
was limited to a positive emotional response, and was therefore
inadequate to describe the counseling situation.

An emotion of either friendliness or hostility, of confidence
or resentment, may make up the relationship, at the beginning
of the contact or later, depending upon many factors. The
above extremes of feeling may not actually be present at the
outset of a given contact but will develop during the course of
the interview. However, since most adults have had some contact with clergymen, the church, and religion, almost everyone
has a predisposition toward one extreme or the other at the outset of a contact, even though this tendency may change later.

I was asked to see a very sick girl by her physician. When I
walked into her room she looked at me and said, "Who are
you?" I said, "I'm the minister of the hospital." She said, "I
don't like ministers." To describe the feeling set up immediately
between us as a lack of friendliness would be an understate-

ment. So long as the feeling is not mutual the ill will or dislike soon gives way to a positive feeling, which happened in the above instance. As soon as I demonstrated to her that I had not come to have a "long" prayer with her, her attitude toward me changed. There came the time when her nurse would send for me instead of for her physician, and for the specific purpose of having a prayer with her. It was not that she disliked ministers, it was only that she did not like her own minister who did two things that upset her; he always reviewed his last Sunday's sermon when he called, which characterized him as a conceited person, and she said he always prayed "an hour." Beyond that she had had trouble with him because of the choir; if it had not been for that trouble the other mistakes might have been forgiven him.

The relationship is all-important in pastoral work. In fact it is the *most* important factor in bringing about healing and in gaining a feeling of emotional security. Much has been written about friendship. The positive relationship is the experience of friendship. A patient I knew over a long and trying period of time said, "I want you to come to me as a friend, not as a minister." The two cannot be separated, however. I would not have had the occasion to see him at all if I had not been a minister. Dr. Samuel Kincheloe of the Chicago Theological Seminary has called the pastor's task, "professionalized friendliness." That is well put providing there is not too much professionalism about it. There should be enough to guard against a sticky and sickly sentimentality, which may develop and prevent healing and growth. That is, the relationship may bog down into an unhealthy emotional dependence which is dangerous, however desired by either one or both persons.

The emotional force, which we call the relationship, is helpful if it is positive. If it is negative, that is, characterized by frustration, distrust, uncertainty, hostility, it is certain to be harmful, unless achieving a short-range goal is considered so desirable that it may be said to be helpful. For example, a counselee may become so angry at the counselor that he goes out and quits a job, or moves away from home, thus resolving another relationship that is destructive. A counselor must be cautious about such short-range objectives, however, for they may not represent true development and may backfire on the counseling relationship, thus doing more harm than good.

The positive emotional force found in the relationship between two or more people is so important for redemptive purposes that I would call it the *Grace of God* at work. It should not be said that this is the only way in which the Grace of God works, but it can be said that it is one, and a very important one. Some may argue that God would not use such poor vehicles as themselves for His Divine Love. God has always used poor vehicles for His Love. Look what our Lord was limited to when he chose His disciples. Most of them failed, so far as history records, but some of them achieved greatness. The shepherd of souls may fail fully, or partially, but fail or succeed there is a power beyond him that works on his side, which he should recognize and come to trust: *the positive emotional relationship* through which flows the healing redemptive love from God. Regardless of the conversational topic if this force is at work redemption is taking place.

The minister, physician, nurse, social worker, teacher, friend, cannot help a person unless a good relationship is established. This is especially true of the minister's work because so much of it lies in the emotional area. There are certain things which a doctor may do for his patient, minor things, like giving a physic, that are not dependent upon affection between the patient and physician. This is not true when it comes to a rapid and satisfactory recovery from an operation; some persons die because the surgeon and his assistants neglect their patients' attitudes. A nurse can make a bed, and do it well without her patient liking her, but her patient's recovery will be retarded by just so much as she is disliked. A social worker may give a client money for relief but if the client is made to feel unworthy, forces of resentment that are far-reaching are set in action. A teacher whose pupils do not like her is a liability and a drag upon education. This feeling of friendliness, or the lack of it, runs through the whole of life and living.

A basic teaching of the Hebrew and Christian religions is that the universe at its heart is friendly. There are few original teachings in the message of Jesus; perhaps His outstanding contribution was His understanding of the Mind and Nature of God. Friendliness, affection, love are the characteristics of God as Jesus described Him. In our own suffering we feel that the world has gone back on us, is indifferent to our suffering or is against us; we have this feeling regardless of how much God through nature is working in our behalf. This attitude toward the Universe, or God, is affected by our feelings for those around us. There is a natural desire within us to feel a kinship with nature and with people; we are naturally friendly. When, through suffering, we turn bitter and resentful it is because we do not have the emotional support which affection gives us. Friendliness renews faith, thus overcoming fear; friendliness as felt between parishioner and minister, expresses confidence through an attitude of "neither do I condemn thee," when the parishioner is suffering from guilt feelings. The parishioner believes that the minister looks at him with the eyes of God, thus he may be relieved more readily by the minister's affection than by anyone else's. The feeling of friendliness, rather than what the pastor says, makes pastoral work helpful in the emotional crisis areas of life as described in Chapter II.

A good relationship is important in pastoral work and preaching because we do not think with our minds, but with our feelings; we are not moved by ideas, but by our emotions; we do not reach decisions with our heads, but with our hearts. Therefore, to influence a person you must have his affection. If a congregation likes its minister he is the greatest preacher in the world; if it dislikes him there is nothing he can do that is commendable, no sermon he can preach that is worth listening to. Some of our reformers might remember that; it is not a question of whether their causes are desirable or not. Rather it is that they are more interested in the cause than in the people it affects.

The relationship develops in proportion to the needs for affection on the part of two people. Its degree is determined by the need for affection and support of those experiencing the contact, for affection *is* support. This need is determined by the stress, or suffering, immediate and past, of the persons sharing in the experience. The surgeon establishes a positive relationship easily and quickly because of the patient's complete dependence upon him. Trust in one's surgeon is a blind, unquestioning trust—it must be, or one would never permit himself to be operated upon. This feeling may be strong only on the patient's part, if the surgeon is interested primarily in the technical job of removing disease through surgery and does not treat the patient as a person with emotional needs, and may lessen when the patient recovers health, remaining quiescent until further need arises.

Religion develops out of man's deep need for fellowship with God, for a satisfactory and satisfying relationship to the world in which he lives. The pastor's task is to aid in working out that relationship. The ancient church fathers thought this role was of vital importance; Protestantism often has not been willing to admit that it is. Clinical psychology, with its pragmatic approach to life, observes every day that man needs and is constantly seeking help in the task of establishing his proper relationship with God and with his environment. He needs help because life is complicated and because suffering disrupts the basic tendency to believe and trust the Universe. Since affection is a stabilizing force, and since the pastor is called to his task and ordained to his role of serving God, the affection which is felt for him may be a unique and soul-strengthening force; to be helpful this affection must be returned by the pastor. I will discuss the pastor's part in the relationship, as to why it becomes creative or destructive, more fully in the following chapter.

A. *Signs of a Positive Relationship*

The tone of voice, the eyes, the face, the head, the content of speech, the hands and the body reveal the nature of the relationship. In America custom dictates that two persons who are introduced shake hands; custom does not dictate whether they shall smile or not, nor what they shall say beyond the introduction. The person who treats you pleasantly, who responds to your interest, who calls you by name, who makes an effort to please you, expresses his goodwill toward you, which indicates that the condition upon which a positive relationship may be built is present. The harsh voice, the abrupt and rude expression, the lack of pleasantness, the failure to shake hands, the indifference to your presence expresses defensiveness and lack of goodwill. A person who is aggressively direct in his speech and manner is on the defensive and may be quite unstable emotionally, just as the "witty" person may be, and any relationship that is established is apt to be superficial and undependable because of the unstable nature of the aggressive person.

B. *Establishing the Relationship*

In pastoral work and personal counseling the relationship is established and strengthened by what the clergyman is able to avoid doing as well as by what he does after the beginning is made. This is one of the most delicate phases of pastoral work, for the minister works from a bias; he is opposed to certain behavior, attitudes, opinions. How to overcome the prejudice engendered by his position in relation to those whose behavior is different and who hold opinions which are at variance with the clergyman's calls for the greatest of skill. Some clergy say frankly they do not care to associate with persons who hold different opinions; we need to remember that our Lord came not to associate with saints alone.

One day I was lecturing before a group of Negro ministers upon the importance of rapport when one of the group got very uncomfortable. Finally he broke in, "How are you going to keep their affection when you got to hurt them?" he asked. "When they do wrong you got to hurt them. That's the way God does." His question is a searching one, perhaps one of the most searching.

When a child does wrong we know we do him no favor, in fact we do him an injustice, in overlooking his act. At the same time if we punish him in anger we do both him and ourselves an injustice. For three years I called upon a thirty-one-year-old man who was very resentful. His bitterness was so intense that his recovery was retarded by it. He blamed another man for the injury which had confined him to his bed and later to a wheel chair and which necessitated one operation after another. He even interviewed an attorney and made plans to sue but never could quite bring himself to the point of starting proceedings. Day after day and week after week I called upon him; time after time he poured forth his bitterness and often he spoke of starting legal action. While I knew of the cause of his injury, I could never believe the accident had been caused either by neglect or malicious intent on the part of the person my friend blamed for his condition. After nearly three years the patient began to improve. One day he said, "You never disagreed with me, I could never have stood that. Neither did you ever agree with me."

We do not have to defend our position by expressing opinions; neither do we have to compromise it. The relationship is strengthened by our genuine interest in a person; that in itself blossoms into affection. Jesus seems, above all others, to have had the ability to attract people to him through his affection for them. His teachings are striking in their simplicity, human in their appeal, but even his teachings vibrate his affection for those around him. He simply loved people into the kingdom.

The building and strengthening of the relationship is slow and tedious and it is only possible when we are afire with love. As God's assistants we serve as the conductor of His love which flows through us like electricity flowing through high-tension wires. Rapport is balanced between the parishioner and his need for help and the pastor and his need to help. When these two needs are met a good relationship is established; if the need for help far outweighs the need to help, pastoral work fails.

IV

THE CLERGYMAN

It is not unusual to have the experience of coming into the presence of someone whose personality, or mind, or manner, causes one's own capacity to express himself to dry up like a stream cut off at its source, while another person will have exactly the opposite effect: one's ideas flow freely through the mind and one's words come forth readily and eagerly. I have never been able to completely understand the reason for this difference. Undoubtedly it turns upon some deep and subtle difference in attitude of mind on the part of someone who can lift us to heights of confidence, thus releasing powers within us, while another confuses and confounds us. In one it is an inherent respect for the personality while in the other it is a subtle desire to dominate and exploit the personality of another. In one it is a feeling of trust and confidence in the Universe, in the other it is a feeling of frustration and restlessness which results in the need to manage and direct others. This in turn is rooted in fear, and that fear is projected upon those he meets, throwing them into confusion and rendering them impotent; while another reassures, encourages, cultivates and stimulates the mind and feelings of those he meets. The one is a destructive, the other a constructive, personality.

One meets these two types of persons everywhere; often not in clear-cut contrast, nor in full development. While often not fully matured and organized in their positions, still most persons, both men and women, fall into one of these two conditions, so far as affecting those they meet is concerned.

I believe this effect upon another personality, subtle and frequently unrecognized by the individual, is ultimately the most important single factor in pastoral work. Therefore we must insist that our students and fellow pastors analyze the kind of relationships they establish in their pastoral contacts. This may necessitate a careful course of counseling with another counselor for themselves, which may or may not mean a character analysis, or a thorough-going psychoanalysis. Theoretically, the latter is desirable, provided an able analyst is available, but that is not possible at present, nor are there prospects of its being possible in the near future for any considerable number of our pastors. If funds were available to make it possible I know an able Christian psychoanalyst who would be willing to give his entire time to analytical examination and instruction of clergymen to enable them to become effective pastors and counselors.

This capacity to permit and assist another personality to be expressive, and therefore creative, is more than the mastery of technique. It turns upon the counselor's deep respect for persons, upon his experience with life, upon the health of his own ego, upon the deep soul, the very self and its development and condition. It has little to do with what one knows and probably little with what one believes; but it has a great deal to do with how one acts in relation to his beliefs.

It has been my experience that some of the greatest religious and intellectual leaders of America, great in that they are well known and have large popular followings, actually have destructive personalities themselves, so that the effect of their meeting other persons individually is to belittle, or lessen, the dignity of those they meet. A part of this effect may be the result of their physical fatigue, a part the frustration of trying to think their way through confused issues, and a part simply because of the large numbers of people they meet, but the sum total, and final conclusion, still adds up to a lack of respect for the personalities of others.

Richard Cabot, one of the most interesting minds that I have ever met, had no such effect upon me and I do not recall that he did upon others, although many held him in great awe, particularly before they met him. Actually I was afraid of him in the early months of our relationship and never, during the entire time of our association together, came to feel so at ease in his presence that I did not treat him with due deference. He was not one to encourage familiarity, for while he was shy and self-conscious, he was also quite conscious of the fact that he was a Cabot, and the Cabots were reputed to have a private line of communication with God. I always suspected that Richard Cabot really believed that. In the first conversation we had together he asked, immediately upon our sitting down, "Why are you interested in sick people?" I replied that I had been seriously ill myself; whereupon he said abruptly, "I'm glad you have." It was years before I understood that what I attributed to bad manners was actually wisdom. Richard Cabot, as a doctor, had learned that suffering is a great teacher. There were times in our relationship when he came close to apologizing, as close as he could come to apologizing for anything, for not having been sick himself; he argued that mental anguish also was a great teacher, a point which I granted a little too readily for his complete satisfaction, for he mentioned it many times upon different occasions.

Richard Cabot, one of the most stimulating doctors of his generation: the man who is the father of medical social work, the discoverer of the clinical pathological conference for medical teaching, the founder of the case-method in medicine, the person whom Paul White of Boston, internationally recognized authority himself upon heart disease, credits with advising investigation which ultimately caused European physicians to come to America to study heart disease—Richard Cabot was always a creative and stimulating listener and thinker so far as my relationship with him was concerned. Just why I do not know. Certainly few men of his generation were more ambitious or worked harder to fulfill their desires. When it came time for him to retire from the Harvard College faculty because of his age he was greatly exercised. He had not thought that such a rule would apply to him. The idea! During the closing weeks of his life he carried on his classes for theological students from his sick bed; when he became too ill to leave his room the students came to him. He did not lack determination nor a will to power. Yet, so far as I can recall, he did not exploit other personalities for his own desires nor did he try to impose his will upon others. He might disagree with what one chose to do, but it was one's right to do it, which did not prevent him from expressing his opinion to the contrary. This expressing of his own view, he believed, was necessary for the integrity of his own personality.

Unfortunately one cannot say the same of many intellectual and spiritual leaders. Most of them seem to think they dare not give attention to another's opinion except to gain information so as to refute it, or to impose their ideas upon others. What happens to the integrity or the dignity of the personality of the person whom they oppose seems not to concern them in the least.

Our Lord said, "Judge not that ye be not judged," and He seemed to have practiced what He taught. This is one of the hardest attainments of all counseling disciplines for in judging others we are judging ourselves, which the counselee fails to recognize. In counseling we are always seeing something of ourselves in others, both what we like as well as what we dislike, and we react accordingly. At heart many of us, if not all, are perfectionists. When we see imperfection in another we express our negative feelings, sometimes in subtle ways and sometimes in crude ways. The subtle is the more damaging, for anyone can identify crudity and compensate for it, but a subtle condemnation creeps into our minds and germinates, coming forth in time as a maggot that has fed upon our souls.

It is the pastor's task to try to clear the maggots from his own soul before spreading them to others. This is done through study, through prayer and meditation, through examining one's own and others' pastoral contacts and their results, but it may have to be done through seeking counseling for oneself and for one's wife. Spiritual maturity and the respect for personality may come only after prolonged suffering and frustration, but it is essential if one is to serve helpfully in the care of souls.

PART TWO

THE ART OF PASTORAL WORK

~~~~~~

V

~~~~~~

CREATIVE LISTENING

THE FIRST PRINCIPLE OF THE DOCTOR IS: *DO NO HARM*. THAT, also, should be the first principle of the clergyman in his pastoral work. We must do as the doctor has done through the generations; we must work as best we can with our present understanding of our task, giving attention to doing as little harm as possible, knowing that God through nature is working on our side. At the same time we must strive to increase our knowledge and understanding of human personality and behavior.

A famous pastor has given us the story of a girl who came to him saying, "Doctor, I want to talk to you about my lack of belief in God." The pastor said, "Tell me first about that love affair." His insight was excellent; his method was poor. He moved too fast. The girl's reaction was certain to have been, "My God, is it that obvious!" Good pastoral work does not shock the parishioner; the risk of doing harm is too great. Hence the importance of sound methods which temper insight.

In my early days as chaplain at the Massachusetts General Hospital in Boston I went about seeing patients suffering from various diseases. Because I did not know what to say, and had little chance to say it even if I had known, I kept quiet and let the patients talk, which they did readily enough. They talked about themselves and their suffering; they talked about their families and homes, and sometimes their lack of family and home; they talked about their jobs and their bosses, jobs they had done and other jobs they hoped to secure; they talked about places they had been, people they had met, books they had read and sometimes books they had written or hoped to write; they talked about sports, baseball, hockey, prize fights, and football; they talked about their churches and their ministers; and again they talked about themselves, their loneliness, their fears, their frustrations, their beliefs and lack of beliefs; they talked of death and of dying, their fear of dying and their eagerness to die. These patients were strangers but a brief time before; now they talked willingly, readily, frankly and eagerly. When I rose to go they thanked me for having helped them. They did seem to have been helped. When I asked myself what I had done the answer was obvious: I had listened.

Psychiatrists, psychoanalysts and social workers have talked of listening. The ancient church made it a Sacrament. Little has been said of it among the free churches since the Reformation. Our clergy have spoken of themselves as "called to preach," by which they have meant proclaiming the gospel, pointing the way. Preaching is preacher-centered while listening is parishioner-centered. Listening means that the sufferer selects the topic of conversation, raises questions, seeks for the answers. Listening means working with a parishioner where *he* is in his soul's journey, not where the pastor is. Listening means patience and courage and trust in the universe of which we are a part. Ministers are usually poor listeners because they have not mastered the art of listening because they have been so on the defensive and because what little instruction they have received in the practical fields has been in the art of preaching, which is the opposite technique to that which makes for effective pastoral work: namely, *listening*.

Underlying listening are the three conditions which were described in Part One: suffering on the part of the parishioner; rapport, which is probably the most important single factor in helpful pastoral care; and the maturity and personhood of the listener. Recognizing these three underlying conditions of listening, let us move on to describe it more specifically as a method. The first time I wrote upon this subject was in *The Art of Ministering to the Sick*. Since then various other authors have written upon the subject calling it by various names, Garrett in *Interviewing: Its Principles and Methods,* Rogers, *Counseling and Psychotherapy,* Bonnell, *Psychology for Pastor and People.* Dr. Carl Rogers has attracted wide attention with his description of what he calls "non directive counseling" and we owe him a debt of gratitude for serving as a corrective against aggression, which is the tendency of everyone who learns to ask questions. At the same time I would maintain that there is no such thing as *non-directive counseling,* for there are many ways of being directive without asking questions. Professor Hocking has said, "All conversation tends to transmit philosophy, since no one can express an idea without conveying, if only by a flick of the eye or a gesture, something of his general temper and outlook, his optimism or pessimism, his belief in intangibles or his hardheaded practicality, his self-centered disdain or his liberal sympathy." [1]

Further, I would maintain that it is the *permissiveness* which exists between the pastor and the parishioner, rather than whether one is directive or not, that is important.

The first phase of the Listening Ministry is *directive listening*.

A. *Directive Listening*

Directive listening is characterized by the use of questions by the pastor. What the scalpel is to the surgeon the question is to the pastoral counselor, and it is quite as dangerous. The good surgical operator is one who knows what to cut and what not to cut, and who has a knowledge of time; the good pastor is one who knows what to ask and what not to ask, plus a feel for timeliness. To ask one's questions too rapidly is like the surgeon who cuts into the abdomen too fast.

The art of pastoral work and counseling is the ability to

[1] Hocking, *Types of Philosophy*, Charles Scribner's Sons, Rev. ed. 1939, p. 5.

know which questions to ask, and when. Through the use of questions we express our interest in a person, we explore his spiritual condition, we relieve suffering, we reveal and aid in the gaining of insight, we release new resources, we stimulate new efforts. The art of asking questions is a major part of the art of pastoral care.

I discovered the use of questions, called psychotherapy, in a state mental hospital while I was still an undergraduate. Shortly after my return to the seminary, a new student, who had returned to finish his preparation for the ministry after spending eight years in business, came to my room. He said, "I heard the boys say you have been studying psychology and counseling. I need some help." We went to work in the way I remembered the psychiatrists asked questions. I asked him why he had left the seminary eight years before, why he had returned, why he went into business, how successful he was in business, why he got married, whether he loved his wife, if they were happily married, why they had a child, and whether his wife was in love with someone else, all in less than half an hour. At the end of that time he jumped up and practically ran out of my room. I did not see him again for a conference for over a week despite his acute need for counseling. That is the way we do harm when, through the use of aggressive questions, we have no consciousness of time. Those were good questions but they should have been spread over a period of several conferences, which would have given rapport and time an opportunity to heal his wounds.

Through the use of questions we explore a person's spiritual condition; at the same time the relationship is developed and insight is gained by the parishioner. The baffling fact remains, however, that some persons are helped through talking about themselves even though little insight is gained.

Directive listening is used when you are seeking to develop a relationship and express your interest in a parishioner. It is used in routine calling, in counseling with youth, in the sickroom, with the bereaved, with persons whom you suspect are having marital difficulty; in this latter situation questions should be asked with care. They are used sparingly in office counseling, especially the first call, for they are apt to carry one off into secondary subjects of discussion. Neither are questions used when the parishioner is talking well, unless you suspect he is simply double-talking himself away from the subject. When a pastoral conference is going well and the subject is opening up nicely, even though there are tears and expressions of hostility, the second phase of the listening ministry is used.

B. *Supportive Listening*

Supportive listening is what I have called passive listening elsewhere, but the term is not adequate for describing what actually happens. *Supportive* is a term now in use by the psychoanalyst—*listening* is my own addition.

In supportive listening the pastor does just what the term implies: he emotionally supports the parishioner as he listens, thus centering attention upon the parishioner's thought and need and not upon something else, for instance, himself, or the church, or Christ. If the parishioner introduces these subjects he discusses them through encouraging the counselee to discuss them, but he does not bring them into the conversation when there is no indication that the parishioner has not thought of them recently himself and unless they are pertinent to the immediate conversation. For too long we have felt that we are being religious only when we are using certain words or discussing certain subjects. I heard of a minister who considered announcing to his congregation that he wanted to talk only about religion when he called upon them. He was completely missing the point. Creative listening as carried on by the pastor, and others, is religion in action, it is overcoming barriers and releasing the resources of God for better and more abundant living as described in the gospels.

Supportive listening is characterized by the pastor's being comparatively passive while the parishioner talks, unfolding his story, taking his time, making his transitions, getting off the subject, weeping, cursing, continuing. It does not mean that the listener goes to sleep, or sits like a hulk; it does not mean, as Seward Hiltner has said, "demonstrating our strength by out-staring the parishioner," by looking him steadily in the eye. It means being alert; it means nodding your head encouragingly; it means looking past the parishioner and out the window or over his head at the wall; it means looking at the parishioner and looking away; it means waiting and hoping; it means relaxing within your physical body so as not to block the story through your own resistance and prejudice; it means trusting God and believing that good can come out of evil and hope out of suffering. Supportive listening is aided by the use of the eyes, the face, the alertness of the body even as it is relaxed, and above all by little grunts of *ah* and *um*, and *um huh*.

Supportive listening is the kind of listening used in the formal confessional. The difference in our use of it and the priest's in the confessional is that confession, as practiced in the liturgical churches, is strictly regulated by canon law and is formalized around the commandments. Thus the priest may not get at the underlying causes of behavior but deals only with the overt act. If, as modern psychology teaches, all behavior is purposeful, then the overt act may be quite insignificant. For example, lying is defensive behavior from the psychologist's point of view. The fact that you have lied is one thing, but the reason for the lie is quite another. From the standpoint of theology a lie is a sin; from the standpoint of psychology it may be the key to an underlying problem which may become serious unless understood and dealt with. Many a mother, upon discovering that her son has lied to her, fears he is headed for the state penitentiary. He *may* be headed for the penitentiary, or the psychopathic hospital, unless the causes of his lying, one link in a chain of behavior, can be examined.

Supportive listening is the method which we use in relieving surface stress in order to get at the underlying causes of behavior, to bring it to the surface of the mind, and to immobilize its emotional force, so that it can be understood and dealt with by the counselee.

C. *Interpretation*

A third phase of the listening method may be called interpretation. Some writers speak of interpretation as a separate method. This seems to me to be a mistake, for the simple reason that without listening there would be nothing to interpret.

Interpretation in pastoral work is a short-cut method and is used primarily because the pastor is pushed for time and because the other phases of his *listening* method have broken down. Sometimes it is necessary to use interpretation because our people have no conception of how they may be helped through pastoral work. They come seeking advice, and advice they expect to receive, because they are accustomed to being told what to do, or because they want the responsibility of a decision to be carried by someone else. In some rare instances advice is desirable for the reason that the responsibility of a decision is too great to be carried by the person needing help.

Interpretation is characterized by the pastor explaining underlying causes of behavior which the parishioner may not be conscious of or understand. It carries certain risks that directive listening does not because the pastor stakes all upon being right in his interpretation and he works upon the assumption that the parishioner will accept it. In this assumption he may be wrong regardless of the truth of his interpretation. A fact may be a fact in reality and to the pastor's knowledge, but unless it is accepted as a fact by the parishioner the pastor must recognize the limitation of its reality and work with the parishioner in his conception of it.

D. *Reassurance*

The fourth phase of the *listening* method is reassurance. This part of the method is so different from the first two types of listening that it, also, is frequently described as a separate method entirely and yet, like interpretation, apart from listening it has little legitimate use. Of the four phases of listening it is least effective and yet of all methods it is used most by clergymen and physicians.

Reassurance is a positive statement by the pastor. It is an expressed opinion that a problem will work itself out or that the pastor believes a parishioner will be able to overcome his suffering. It is encouragement. The limitation of reassurance is not in its desirability but in our failure to bring the encouragement desired when we reassure people. A person will not have courage because we tell him to, but he can be helped to develop courage through our listening to him, through our interest in him and through our own courage. Then we can tell him he has courage as *we observe he has taken heart again*: that is reassurance.

As a method, reassurance should be used sparingly. It must be expressed simply if it is to be effective. The more words used while reassuring a person the weaker becomes the statement. Small words are the strong words; in attempting to reassure a person use simple terms and be certain that your voice and manner reveal that you mean them.

Reassurance, for the Protestant, is what the statement of absolution is for the Catholic, psychologically. "I absolve you in the name of the Father and the Son and the Holy Ghost," is the Catholic statement following confession. The statement of reassurance is, "I believe you will be all right"; "I can see a lot of hope in your case"; "I have faith this will not throw you." "There is no such thing as being ruined except as you think you are, and you don't think so in this case"; "I believe in you and I'm going to see you through." A soul-companion never condemns, never judges, but always attempts to aid.

You will note in the above statements of reassurance that the Catholic absolution is pronounced in the name of the Trinity, while the Protestant reassurance is pronounced in the name of the pastor and personalized around him. This is an advantage in that it is intimate and personal; it is a disadvantage in that it is human and thought of as human by the parishioner. The Protestant's reassurance is limited in that it lacks the perspective, the far view, the support of the Creator Himself.

In our book, *The Art of Ministering to the Sick,* Dr. Cabot wrote a chapter that is often accredited to me, entitled, "The Two Must Face a Third"; namely the parishioner and pastor must face God. I agree. I also recognize that, because of the lack of belief in God of many of our people, it is impossible to face the Third. Many of our clergy in their attempt to be helpful wander off into pious platitudes, only to have their reassurance fail. Two can face God when both know God; when one knows God the other may gradually come to know Him but it is a slow process and not brought about through an easy statement or exhortation. It is brought about through the slow, persistent, affectionate demonstration of the nature of God.

If I were told I could have but one method in pastoral work I would choose the *listening* method. Let us illustrate it further in its various phases through an example taken from actual pastoral work. The illustration is authentic. Note that the pastor uses all four phases of the listening method in a single pastoral conference. Note also the pastor's partial failure in the early sessions of his work with Mrs. Loucks. In another sense it was not failure because his relationship was building up steadily, which enabled his work to be helpful as it was in the end.

VI

CREATIVE LISTENING, Continued

IN THE FOLLOWING CALLS WE SEE THE METHODS OF *LISTENING* illustrated. This is the verbatim report of several calls made by a pastor. The editorial comments are in italics.

PRELIMINARY DESCRIPTION: I call regularly in the local hospital, near which my church is located, so that I know the hospital staff well. The doctors and nurses frequently ask me to see patients who are not receiving other pastoral care.

One afternoon when I stopped to speak to a head nurse she asked if I knew a Mrs. James Loucks. When I told her I did not she said, "I believe she would enjoy having you come in. She has cancer—and knows she cannot live." The nurse took me to the room and introduced me as a minister who called upon many of the patients in the hospital.

First call, March 31:

I said, "Good morning, Mrs. Loucks."

She smiled, and answered, "Good morning. What shall I call you? Father?"

"Most of my friends and parishioners call me *Mister* Beal, but you may address me as you prefer."

"I prefer to call you Mr. Beal."

"What is your church?"

"I am Episcopal, but I was born in a Catholic home. I married an Evangelical, and we compromised and joined the Episcopal Church."

"Your husband is Evangelical?"

"Yes, I am well acquainted with the Evangelical people. I was in your hospital over in St. Louis. We lived not very far from there. I know the Reverend Dr. Blank very well. His son is a minister near here and has been in our home a number of times. We went to church there too, but most of the services were in German and I couldn't understand them."

"Have you lived here long?"

"About five years. You see, there is no Episcopal Church here, so I have attended other churches, but I do not belong to a local church. A minister stopped here recently and spoke to me. He had a long prayer with me, and it scared me. I dreamed about it."

"What did you dream?" (*He is following his leads closely.*)

"Oh, horrible things. You see, I have a cancer. I have been operated on three times; I know I cannot get well, and those dreams scare me."

"Did you ever have pleasant dreams?" (*He fails to follow the lead, she is talking about "a horrible dream," while he shifts to "pleasant dreams" in an effort to become more positive in his call. This is a mistake here for he is changing the subject. This is a first call; therefore he should let the patient take it where she wishes. He might have inquired, "Why did they frighten you?" or "They were unpleasant dreams?"*)

"Yes, I have had one wonderful dream. I told it to my daughter as best I could. I have never told it to anybody else because they might think I am bugs. It's hardly a dream. I wouldn't know what to call it. I was in a coma, I guess. Oh, I was awake; still, I was asleep. I guess I was dead. The place I was—well, I just can't describe it. It was so beautiful. There were men and women there, too, but you couldn't tell the difference. They were bodies and they weren't bodies. They were just spirits, dressed in white. And their faces, I could recognize their faces. It was just so beautiful, I can't describe it."

"Has that dream helped you in any way?"

"Yes, it has. I am not afraid to die and I know that, when I die, I'll be there right away. That can't be purgatory. That must have been heaven."

"Then you are confident that you will go there?" (*Again, he is too aggressive. This is like a challenge. Greater passivity would have been desirable.*)

"I am not worried about it at all. The only thing that I am worried about is my littlest daughter just twelve. But I shouldn't worry about her. I have no reasons to worry. She is well taken care of. She has so much love. No, I don't worry." (*One would doubt the truth of this response because of the "horrible dreams" mentioned earlier. This is a first call upon a complete stranger and we should not expect it to accomplish everything.*)

Just then her husband came in. She turned to him and said, "I am telling the minister about that wonderful experience. Mr. Beal, meet my husband." After the introduction, I spoke a few words with her husband. The nurse came in with Mrs. Loucks' dinner. I rose and excused myself, saying I would see her again soon.

"I do so much appreciate the fact that you came to see me. As soon as you have a little leisure, won't you please come back?"

"Thank you. I will. Good-bye."

Second call, April 6:

I went to the third floor and inquired about Mrs. Loucks. The nurse told me she wanted to see me. We went into the room. We noticed another woman standing at the bed. The nurse said:

"Mrs. Loucks, here is the minister to see you," then left the room.

"I am so glad to see you," Mrs. Loucks said, smiling.

"Mrs. Loucks should not have any company," the visitor said.

Mrs. Loucks said, "But I am glad that you are here. Won't you sit down?"

"Her husband told me not to let anyone in," the visitor persisted.

I said to Mrs. Loucks, "I will be back to see you in the morning."

The visitor said sternly, "But her husband does not want anyone to see her."

"Good-bye, Mrs. Loucks," I said.

"Come back in the morning," Mrs. Loucks said as I left. (*This was the best way to handle a difficult situation which might have become more embarrassing.*)

Third call, April 7:

Afternoon. When I came to the nurse's desk she said, "Mrs. Loucks has been asking for you. I just came from her room."

"Is the other lady there who was present yesterday?" I asked.

"No, no one is with her." I went into the room.

"Good afternoon, Mr. Beal. I was afraid you wouldn't come back."

"Why would you think I would not come back?"

"Because of the way that woman talked yesterday."

"Who was she?"

"Not even a relative, but she assumes charge when she comes. I don't want to see her and I don't want her to run my affairs."

"You were Catholic in your childhood, were you not?" (*This seems like a rapid shift. It is an effort to explore her religious outlook.*)

"Some of my family was, but I wasn't. After we married, we joined the Episcopal Church when we lived in a suburb near Chicago, and I have kept my membership there ever since."

"How long have you lived here?"

"About five years, but we have moved around from place

to place for the last fifteen years. This is about the longest we have ever been in one place. We have never brought our membership to a church here, but we live with a son-in-law who belongs to St. John's. We are a very clannish family. When I got sick three years ago, we sold our home and all the children wanted us to live with them, but I chose this one. My son-in-law is a wonderful person. You may know him. Of course, they don't go to church very much. You know young people are worldly."

"Does your husband go to church?"

"No, he is the manager of his business and he works very hard; he usually rests on Sunday mornings."

"The vision you told me about the other day is most interesting." (*Again, this is a rapid shift, even though it brings good results.*)

"It is a great comfort to me, because I know that I cannot get well."

"What makes you think that you cannot get well?"

"I have cancer and I know it."

"Has the doctor told you that you will not get well?" (*Good question.*)

"No one has. But last Christmas, when the children were together and I had just come home from the hospital, I told them that we might as well be happy this year, because, 'next Christmas at this time your mother will not be with you.' "

"So you are quite certain that you will not get well?" (*This is laboring the point, probably because he can think of nothing else to say.*)

"I am certain of that. I don't know just why I am certain. This is cancer. I have had two removed, and I know I can't get well."

"Is your faith sufficient to meet your needs?" (*This is what the minister wants to know, but his question is too aggressive. She will tell him the answer only when she is ready to, and she should not be forced to talk about it before she is ready. In this instance, she is not ready, so she does not tell him.*)

"I think it is. I am a funny person though. Do you think it is right for a church to have bingos and dancing?" (*There is doubt in her mind. The conversation takes a peculiar turn because she does not want to talk further about his question.*)

"What do you think about them?"

"I think that it is wrong. They say they do it to keep the young people together. Do you do those things in your church?"

"No, we don't, but don't you think that is a matter of opinion?"

"I guess it is, but I don't like it. I don't say these things to other people. I don't want them to think I'm 'nuts.' That's why I don't tell others about my vision. I wish I could remember the words. My daughter said, 'Mother, you should have called a nurse and told her to write it down.' But the nurse would have thought I was 'nuts.' "

I noticed she was rather weak; I thought it best to terminate the interview. She asked me to come back tomorrow. I told her I would. (*He should have had prayer at the close of his interview. The indications are: 1, They had talked about the church, and she had indicated her interest in the church; 2, The rapport was good. When a person permits himself to like a minister, he is not antagonistic nor indifferent toward religion.*)

Fourth call, April 10:

The supervisor of nurses telephoned me to say that Mrs. Loucks would like to have me see her. As I came to the floor the supervisor told me that Mrs. Loucks was quite depressed this morning. As I entered the room, she was crying.

"Good morning, Mrs. Loucks," I said.

"Good morning, Mr. Beal. I am so glad you came. If I can quit crying, I want to talk to you."

"What causes you to cry this morning?" I asked. (*In such a situation it is best just to wait it out. She will talk as soon as she can, so why push her?*)

"It is the restlessness and the pain. I wish you would pray for me. Last night one of the nurses came in the room and she prayed with me. It was wonderful, Mr. Beal. It gave me such peace of mind and heart. I wish you would pray for me, too, and read to me from the Scripture. When I was a child, I didn't get to know the Scriptures. The Bible has such wonderful promises."

"Did the nurse read to you from the Scriptures also?"

"No, she didn't, but I wish you would."

"I will be pleased to do that, but would you rather talk a little first or shall we have our Scripture and prayer now?"

"My faith is like yours. It was a mistake that my husband and I went to another church. I have been associated with your kind of people so much. My babies were born in a Deaconess Hospital, and here the nurses are so noble, and they are mostly all girls of your faith. I am going in to church IF I GET WELL. My son-in-law belongs to St. John's, and the children go there. We could all be happy there together."

"Then you feel that you are satisfied with your faith?"

"Yes, I am. If you will be kind enough to read to me and pray with me?" Whereupon I quoted to her from the Psalms and prayed with her.

"Thank you. I feel at ease now. I think I am going to sleep." I left the room.

Fifth call, April 11:

As I came to the floor where Mrs. Loucks is a patient the supervisor told me that she wished I would call on Mrs. Loucks.

As I came in the door Mrs. Loucks spoke, "Good morning, Mr. Beal. I feel so much better this morning. Those were just like words from heaven that came to me yesterday from your lips, and I have been praying and thinking ever since. I have been such a selfish person in my lifetime. I never permitted my children to play with the neighbors, and I never cared to associate with other people. I always considered myself so much better than they, and our family was better than others. But I have made up my mind that, if I get well, I am going to live differently. I am going to do things for other people and not be so clannish and so selfish."

"Have you told that to God in your prayers?" (*He fails to follow the lead about "clannishness and selfishness." In fact, he needed to say nothing but "Hummmm."*)

"Yes, I have, and I have been praying in my own words too. I used to always chant my prayers rather fast, and God seemed so far away I couldn't touch Him. But now God seems very near to me, since I told Him how selfish I was and that I am going to change my life, if I get well, and live differently."

"But you have told me that there is no chance for you to get well." (*This was definitely a low blow. One should not be annoyed because a person cannot make up her mind, whether it is about death, or getting married, or whatever the subject; when we criticize a person, as this question does, we shame him and thus ruin our opportunity to be helpful.*)

"I felt that way about it, when I came into the hospital. I haven't eaten anything for two weeks, but today I feel differently. I told the nurse to bring me some spinach. I want to start eating. I feel now that I have reason to live." (*This is a sign of a sense of guilt, for the desire for punishment is an indication of guilt. Of course, I suppose some people like spinach, but until certain I would interpret the eating of it as a feeling of guilt.*)

"If I get well, I am going to get active in the church. I used to go to a church and slip out so no one would speak. I didn't want to speak to them. The ladies would ask me to join the organizations. And I have been very selfish with my husband too. I never wanted him to associate with other men and make friends, because I thought they weren't good enough. In my giving, too, I have tried to give what I thought I should. My mother taught us to tithe, but I have not been giving what I know I should have been giving. I have been very selfish." (*A feeling that others are not as good as oneself or family is an indication of guilt feelings. It turns upon an effort to stand aloft because one dare not associate with sinners.*) "If I get well, things are going to be different." (*The above may be considered a confession. We must be certain that a confession is complete. It may be tested with a further question about some statement contained in the confession, as "How long have you felt you have been selfish?"*)

"So you feel more at ease now than you did?"

"Indeed I do, and there is some more of the vision that comes to me that I want to tell you about. When I went to the stream, I had a basket of flowers on my arm, and each of these flowers was a soul. I looked across the river to the most beautiful place. I can't describe it. And there were men and women there too. I recognized some of them, but I won't tell them, because they would be afraid they were going to die. You see, I didn't cross the river. I was on this side, I wasn't dead. It was so beautiful. I noticed that the flowers wilted in the basket when I started back home."

Her husband came in at this time and greeted me. She asked him if he had met me and we said that we had met. She started to tell her husband how much better she was this morning and what the quoting of the Scriptures and the prayer meant to her. She asked me for the references of the Scriptural quotations. Fortunately, I did remember which Psalm it was that I had quoted and what words of Jesus. Then she asked if I would read and pray with her again. I did. Her husband thanked me also and offered to pay me for coming. I told him that I accept no gratuities for pastoral calls. They both invited me to come back.

Sixth call, April 15:

When I inquired about Mrs. Loucks' condition of the nurse,

she said that the patient was suffering quite a bit. The nurse said that I should see Mrs. Loucks because she was expecting me. I went into the room.

"Hello, Mrs. Loucks," I said.

"Hello, Mr. Beal. I have missed you. I am so glad you came."

"Have you been resting easier?"

"I have suffered a lot, but I have been taking pain killers and that makes it easier, but I believe I am prepared to go."

"Why do you say that?"

"Because I don't know if it was wicked or not, but yesterday morning that old man across the hall died, and I prayed that I might go too. Do you think that was wicked?"

"And what do you think about it?"

"I don't think it was, because I want to die now."

"And you feel that you are ready now to die?" (*This was well done.*)

"Yes, I do, since the other day."

"What do you mean by 'since the other day'?"

"Since I found out how selfish I was and made my confession. I feel better about it now, and I am no longer worried. Do you think I should be worried?" (*He might have inquired, "Are you still worried?" If she is, he will know that her confession was not complete. The fact that she even raises the question should make one suspicious that there was something more she wished to talk about.*)

"Didn't you feel a lot better, when you made your confession and decision? Did you feel that God was very near you?"

"Yes. Will you read to me and pray with me again?" I quoted the 23rd Psalm and had prayer with her. I started to leave. She called, "Come back again. Will you?"

"Yes, I will, and if you want me before I get back again, tell the nurse. She will call me. I am always pleased to visit with you."

After the call I spoke with the nurse, who told me that Mrs.

Loucks was very low and undoubtedly would suffer terrifically were it not for the narcotics.

Seventh call, April 27:

I had been to see Mrs. Loucks a number of times but found her either asleep or delirious. Once she sent for me but when I came she said she was too ill to talk but asked for a prayer. Today she was conscious and asked the nurse to call me. The nurse told me she was very low. I went into the room.

"Good morning, Mrs. Loucks," I said.

"I sent for you yesterday, but the nurse said you were not here. I was sinking and thought I was dying. I want you here by me when I die."

"Why do you want me here?" (*This seems cold blooded. She is making a reasonable request. However, his method produces results.*)

"Then I won't be afraid."

"Why are you afraid?"

"Oh! It's such a great adventure. I had a dream yesterday. I was down by the river again, but I was so weak I could not make it across the river. I tried, but I could not get across."

"What did you do then?"

"I awoke. That is when I wanted you. I want to be sure I can get across the river. I am not a loose woman. I don't mean that, but I want to be sure that I get across. Do you think I will?"

"What makes you doubt you will not?"

"I wonder if my confession is enough. I know I have been a sinful woman."

"Have you prayed since you made your confession?" (*He failed to follow his lead.*)

"I have. Will you make a confession for me? You can say it like I mean it. Make a confession for me."

"Wouldn't you rather say it yourself?"

"I do confess, when I pray."

"Don't you think God knows you and hears your confession?"

"Yes. But I want you to confess for me."

"Dear Father in heaven, through Christ my Saviour, I, a poor sinner, acknowledge and deplore my many sins and wickedness which I have committed against Thee by thought, word, and deed. If we confess our sins, He is willing and righteous to forgive us our sins and cleanse us from all unrighteousness. I come to Thee at this time imploring Thy forgiveness and grace. I am not worthy to be called Thy child; make me as one of Thy hired servants."

"Say that again for me."

"I am not worthy to be called Thy child; make me as one of Thy hired servants. Thou dost open Thine arms and receive me, as a father pitieth his children. Come unto me all ye that labor and are heavy laden and I will give you rest. Forgive me, heavenly Father, and receive me. Amen. . . . Is this your sincere confession?"

"It is, Mr. Beal."

"Then hear these words of absolution. . . . Him that cometh to me I will in no wise cast out. As a minister of our Lord, Jesus Christ, I announce to you, who sincerely repent and heartily believe, the forgiveness of your sins in the name of the Father, the Son, and the Holy Ghost. Be it unto you according to your faith. Amen."

"Oh, thank you, thank you so much." She held my hand to her face as she thanked me.

"Do you think you will still be afraid?" I asked.

"I don't think so," she said.

"Good-bye, Mrs. Loucks. I'll see you again soon."

"Good-bye. Please do."

Eighth call, April 30:

I have tried to see Mrs. Loucks each day, but have found her sleeping or so confused the call was ineffective. Today I found her able to talk.

"Good evening, Mrs. Loucks."

"I am glad you came. I am so weak today. Will you please hand me the tissues. They fell to the floor."

"The box is empty. But here is another one."

"I can't get them out of that box."

"Shall I take them out and put them in this larger one?"

"Yes, please do."

"Can you reach them here?"

"Yes. Thank you. . . . (*pause*) . . . I am still worried."

"What are you worried about?"

"I am a sinful woman."

"Why do you say that?"

"I wonder if my confession has been deep enough."

"Do you feel that it hasn't been deep enough?"

"Yes, I do."

"Is there anything you would like to tell me?"

"I have committed a great sin."

"Do you want to tell me about it?"

"I caused a . . . " I could not hear what she said.

"Did you say you caused a divorce?"

"No, an abortion—an abortion. And that is murder, isn't it?"

"What do you think about it?" (*Good question. It lets the patient talk further.*)

"I was young, and you know how young people are—young married people. I didn't want to bother with a child. Young girls in those days did it. I went to a doctor. He charged me fifty dollars. But I let him do what he wanted to do."

"Was the pregnancy well advanced?"

"About six months. I was taken to a hospital and hovered between life and death. But I recovered. It was murder. I know it was murder. It has haunted me ever since. Do you think God will ever forgive me?"

"Did you say it has haunted you ever since?"

"Yes, and I don't know what to do about it. I don't know the Bible. What should I do about it?"

"Do you believe that God loves you?" (*Good question. Leads toward reassurance.*)

"I believe that He does. But I have done this awful thing."

"Have you ever prayed to Him about it?"

"Yes, I have."

"What have you told God about it?"

"I have told Him what a mistake I made. I was young then and didn't realize what I was doing. I am so ashamed of myself. But it was murder."

"Do you know the Lord tells us that if we repent and believe He is willing to forgive us?" (*Now the pastor begins his reassurance, but he is careful to be certain that the patient understands his statement and accepts the reassurance.*)

"Will He forgive anything?"

"If you were God and one of your children was as sorry over a sin as you are, would you be willing to forgive your child?"

"Yes, I would. I would do anything now to undo that murder."

"Don't you think God knows your heart now and is willing to forgive you too?"

"Oh, how grateful I will be, if He will forgive me."

"Have you ever heard the Scripture, 'Though your sins be as scarlet, they shall be white as snow, though they be red like crimson, they shall be as wool'?"

"Say it again, Mr. Beal." I did.

"Will you pray for me?" I prayed. (*Unfortunately, the pastor does not report his prayer for us. This should have been a prayer of triumph and of confidence—a prayer for forgiveness.*) After the prayer she said, weakly, "I am finished now. You help me. Won't you come back?"

"Yes. Good-bye. I hope you rest better tonight."

Ninth call, May 4:

Mrs. Loucks had been sleeping each day when I called until today. The nurse called me and said that Mrs. Loucks had been asking for me all morning. I went to the hospital at once.

"Hello, Mrs. Loucks, I haven't forgotten you, but you have been sleeping each day."

"I am so glad you came. You have been so kind to me."

"Is there anything that I can do for you?"

"Can you tell me if it is wrong for me to pray that I might die? I have been praying that the Lord would take me home. I am no longer afraid. I know He has forgiven me. I feel it for certain and now my body is so weary that I long to be with Him. Is it wrong for me to pray that He will take me?"

"Since you feel that you are ready to go, I am sure that it isn't wrong." (*Good statement of reassurance.*)

"I know that He has forgiven me and now I look forward to the time when I can be with Him and see my mother and my sisters. I know it must be a beautiful place and I can hardly wait. Won't you pray for me too, that I might soon be relieved?"

"Are you resting better now?"

"Yes. I have nothing to worry me any more. The Lord has lifted my feet on higher ground, and I am so thankful to Him. And now I will keep still. I am so tired. Will you pray for me?" I prayed for her. (*Again, we would like to know the content of his prayer. I think she makes a legitimate request. I have prayed upon several occasions that a person might be taken "home," including a petition in such a prayer that, "strength may be given that she may complete the race so nobly run.")*

"Good-bye, Mrs. Loucks."

"Don't forget me in your prayers."

Final note: Mrs. Loucks died peacefully that afternoon. She asked her family to leave, and after I prayed with her she said she wanted to sleep. She died a little later, never regaining consciousness. I conducted her funeral two days later.

Editor's Summary: Here we see an interesting pastoral assignment and the use of the listening ministry. The fact that Mrs. Loucks was not one of the minister's own parishioners did not appreciably affect his work with her.

The striking thing in this series of calls is that the pastor made many mistakes, but because he persisted and was faithful in his calling and because Mrs. Loucks was suffering severely, in the end he was able to gain peace for her through God's Grace. I would criticize the pastor for not following his leads more closely; while he was attempting to use the listening method, but he bungled it badly at places.

These calls reveal clearly the significance of the pastor's work and the importance of permitting a suffering person to talk. No amount of reassurance, the quoting of Scripture, and prayer, would have relieved this woman. She had to make a confession. How much her early training had to do with this desire I do not know.

It is interesting that the pastor thought repeatedly that all was well with Mrs. Loucks only to find that it was not. Gradually as a greater confidence in the minister built up, as she suffered more, as Scripture and prayer revealed more of the Nature and Mind of God, she was enabled to complete her confession and gain peace. In spite of much fumbling, and a too aggressive handling of the situation, this should be listed as successful pastoral care.

VII

PRAYER

A WOMAN TOLD ME OF HER FEELING OF "ALONENESS." SHE could not pray, she said, and feel any warmth of fellowship in her prayer although she has always been a devoted mother and an active church member. At the time she told me this story she was in a state of nervous and physical exhaustion. A son and daughter had died five years before. When I inquired how long she had felt this barrenness in her devotional life she began to speak of a tragedy which had happened sixteen years ago when a car her son was driving turned over and killed the young daughter of a clergyman. Despite the son's efforts to alleviate the family's suffering the minister had felt deep resentment and had threatened to kill the lad. Since that time she had not been able to pray with any degree of satisfaction.

In time of personal crisis many people lose their way religiously and, having lost their way, their personal crisis deepens, for they have nothing to support them. Most people take their faith for granted and go along fairly well until something happens to them. Then they cannot pray effectively. They cannot pray because they do not really believe in God, or understand the purpose of prayer. All too often God is thought of as a glorified errand boy, who cometh when we say come and goeth when we say go.

Prayer is man's effort to release resources in his behalf which are beyond his own control. The basic question concerning prayer is, does it help? Does it release new resources? Does prayer increase God's interest in us and our struggles? Here is a child who is dying and the parents request the pastor's prayers; here is a man facing life with a handicap and the pastor comes to pray with him; here is a girl whose heart is broken because of a frustrated love affair; here is a person who is ill, another who thinks his life is a failure; here is a man who feels guilty; here is a woman who is lonely; here is one whose business is failing. Will prayer help? Will they find in prayer the answer to their needs?

Prayer will help; but it may not help in the specific way that often is desired by the supplicant.

Will prayer change God's Mind? *It will not.*

God's Mind does not need to be changed. It is Sufficient and Creative. Prayer changes our own minds. It brings us into close touch with the Creative Mind of God and strengthens us. Many a person dies who prays for health and many a person is hurt who prays for safety. But the person who prays for health honestly and in humility, assists the health-giving resources already within his body which is God at work. The person who prays for safety is conscious of danger and therefore is more alert and wisely cautious than another.

Prayer, especially the prayer which is prayed by one standing beside us who is free from the heat of the suffering, reminds us of the things we have forgotten and causes us to relax our desires into Greater Desires than our own. It helps us to gain perspective and see that the limited vision we have of ourselves is not the whole of our living. Prayer helps us to trust the world in which we live; to trust the people about us, the chairs upon which we sit, the ground upon which we walk, the day with its work and the night that gives us rest. Especially it helps us as we see other trusting people who pray.

When all this is said and done there is still much of mystery in prayer.

I was told of an American soldier in Australia who had a moronic urge to kill civilian women. After the third murder he was apprehended. When he was brought before the military authorities he said, "That's what I was sent over here for. To kill people!" When it was pointed out that he was not sent to Australia to kill civilian women but enemy soldiers he failed to see the point. He was tried and sentenced to be hanged. The chaplain saw him regularly, ministering to him up to and including the time of his execution. When it was over the chaplain said to his superior officer, "When I die, I hope I'll go to as happy a heaven as that man went to." There is Christian faith! There is the mystery of religion, the mystery of God's redeeming power that may be released through prayer.

Prayer fails when we attempt to bend the powers of the universe to our desires; it helps when we bring ourselves into line with its creative forces. The pastor will do well not to use the phrase, "Thy will be done," in his pastoral work. This phrase probably is the most misunderstood one in the whole New Testament. If we pray, "Thy will be done" with a sick person he is apt to think we are giving God permission to take him; when we pray, "Thy will be done" with a person who is sick and he dies, the family is sure God killed him and they rather think we had a part in it; while if we pray, "Thy will be done" with a broken-hearted girl she is certain to think God did not approve of her love. There are other ways of bringing a parishioner into touch with God through prayer than through using this phrase.

A further objection to it is that people are constantly dying when it is not God's will, otherwise why the tremendous resources for health, for happiness, for affection and friendliness which are within us? We have but to recognize that since 1900 approximately twenty years have been added to the life expectancy of every person through the advances of medical science. Why would God desire that we should live twenty years longer now than He willed a half century ago? To believe that there is a specific time and place for dying for every person is just nonsense, and yet this is the most commonly held view concerning death that one faces among Christian and non-Christian people alike. To believe it is God's will that we suffer because we have sinned is a false assumption. Suffering is an instrument of God for creative growth, not an end in itself for punishment. It often is the pastor's task to interpret suffering to the sufferer; to help him discover how suffering may be turned into triumphant living even as our Lord turned suffering into victory.

In his use of prayer in pastoral work the minister should always strive for quietness within himself. This is best achieved through physical relaxation. Thus the same condition is suggested to the parishioner. The tone of voice should be modulated, easy, natural. Why so many of our clergy feel they must pray in a pious, other-worldly tone is incomprehensible; one wonders if they think God does not understand a quiet, natural voice. This tendency grows out of a desire to suggest awe through the voice; it suggests spiritual nausea rather than awe to most sensible people. Naturalness, dignity, quietness are the characterizations of effective pastoral prayer.

The prayer should never be long—about the number of phrases that are contained in the twenty-third Psalm is the desired length. It is surprising how we come to have a feel for the length of a prayer as well as for its content when we ourselves are in a prayerful mood.

Dr. Henry Sloane Coffin has said that public prayer should be cast in the language of religion, and that the language of religion is the language of lyric poetry. The little words are the strong words; simple phrases carry the heaviest loads. Not all ministers are poets nor can all master a simple language of expression for use in their public prayers. It was for this reason that I prepared the little book, *Comfort Ye My People* (Macmillan Company). The prayers need not be read in the pastoral situation but they are suggestive of phrases and ideas which have been found to be helpful.

Following are a few sample prayers.

Prayer in a Home

Eternal God, Father of us all;
Thou who hast blessed us through love and affection,
We give Thee thanks for homes and the joys of home;
We give Thee thanks for these Thy children;
Continue to bless them and make them strong in faith.
Bless the husband and father, the wife and mother
Of this home. Through their love for each other
May they know Thy love for them.
Bless the son and daughter of this home, and
May they know the joys of men and women as they know the joys of
    youth.
We pray for homes less fortunate;
May we be mindful of our neighbors and serve them as they have
    served us.
We pray for the church, family of families, and home of homes,
United in love for Thee, through Jesus Christ, our Lord. *Amen.*

Prayer of Thanksgiving upon the Birth of a Child

Almighty and Everloving Father, Creator and Sustainer of life,
We give Thee thanks for the joys of living, and for the strength of
    health,
For the safe care of this one, we thank Thee,
We rejoice in the affection of this mother and father,
New life from their lives, new strength and faith and hope;
Bless this child, O God, and make it Thine own.
We remember that our Lord came into the world as a child,
We know the joy His mother knew as she held Him in her arms.
As we share the mother's joy so we know the father's hope;
Strengthen this mother and father in their parenthood,
And may their affection overflow into this new life;
Grant them health and faith for the day's task, through Jesus Christ,
    our Lord. *Amen.*

Prayer for One Who Is Ill

Eternal Father, Thou Who art near unto us at all times,
We give Thee thanks for the gift of life and the strength of faith;

In hard moments we turn to Thee, in lonely moments Thou art our
companion;
We thank Thee for doctors and nurses, and all who serve Thee through
the healing ministries,
We remember our loved ones, strengthen them and keep them safe.
Bless this one, give him quietness of soul and ease from pain,
And make strong the forces of health within him;
May he know the support of the Everlasting Arms
And the confidence of the Everlasting Hope.
Through Jesus Christ, our Lord. *Amen.*

Prayer for a Bereaved Family

Lord and Father of us all,
We give Thee thanks for life and the joys of life,
We give Thee thanks for faith and the hope of faith.
Thou hast taught us to love Thee through Thy love for us,
We rest in Thee.
In this hour we rest in Thy support,
And we know the strength of the Everlasting Arms——
We rest our loved one in Thee.
That one who is near unto us in affection,
Now is with Thee; may we gain comfort from the thought.
Strengthen this family, the mother, and these children,
And may they find comfort in Thee.
May we remember it is but a short time
Until we too will pass along this way to be reunited with our
loved ones.
We pray in the name of Jesus Christ, our Lord. *Amen.*

The hardest single decision the minister faces in his use of
prayer in pastoral work is in knowing when to pray. While this
is a decision that must be made in each situation there are
principles that can serve as guides in reaching the decision.
These principles have been gleaned from observation in clinical pastoral experience.

The major situations in which the pastor will use prayer are:
(1) with the bereaved; (2) with older people; (3) with the
sick. In pastoral counseling, which is conducted in the minis-

ter's office, one may or may not have prayer with a counselee. Dr. Philip Guiles, Professor of Pastoral Psychology at Andover-Newton Theological Seminary and Assistant to the Pastors at Old South Church, Boston, where he has carried on this kind of a ministry for many years, has said that he may have prayer regularly with a counselee during the early periods of a conference, but then he stops until the basic problems have been worked out, after which he again introduces the practice, carrying on definite instruction in an understanding of prayer and the spiritual life. He follows this practice because prayer helps the people who come for counseling to accept him as a minister and develops the proper relationship; he believes that if it were continued during the exploratory part of his work with a counselee it would block the discovery process and suppress certain material that needs to come out. It must be remembered that Dr. Guiles does more work of a depth nature than most ministers even in office pastoral counseling will do.

In ministering to the bereaved one will always have prayer at the end of the first call and usually for several calls thereafter. However, if one then moves into a more formal type of pastoral counseling, such as I believe we must do in some instances, the use of prayer may be dropped, lest certain dynamic material of an unpleasant nature be suppressed, such as feelings of hostility toward the dead person, about which the counselee feels guilty.

Older people will expect the minister to read their Bibles and have prayer with them, especially if they are shut-in. They will also be greatly helped by having him bring them communion. Some ministers are now purchasing wire-recorders which enable them to take a record of the communion service as it is conducted in their own church to the shut-in; they cannot go to church so the church comes to them.[1]

In ministry to the sick the question of knowing when to pray and when not to pray becomes more difficult. With one's

[1] See *Older People and the Church*, Maves and Cedarleaf.

own parishioners I would list the following situations as those
in which the minister would always pray, unless some very unusual factor clearly indicated that a prayer would be harmful:
(1) *Before a surgical operation.* The time to make this call is
the night before the operation, as the pre-operative technique
carried on the morning of the operation is quite involved, and
the patient is so caught up in it that the minister's prayer is
ineffective if he arrives shortly before the operation is sched-
uled; while the night before is a hard time for a patient.

(2) Following the birth of a baby. When a young mother
realizes that life has actually come from her life she comes the
nearest to worshipping in its purest sense that she ever experiences. The exception will be the mother who resents her pregnancy and rejects the baby. In that case a mother may express
feelings of hostility which need pastoral or psychiatric attention.

(3) When facing life with a physical handicap. This is an
inner-personal problem of one's relationship with his God and
his universe. Prayer again may suppress feelings of hostility or
it may be the way in which those feelings are opened up and
expressed. There are few things a handicapped person cannot
do if he works out his inner feelings and if those around him
permit him to develop his capacities: the great problem is one
of accepting the handicap, which he can be helped to do
through prayer.[2]

(4) When one is in prolonged pain or is going through a
long convalescence. These two situations are quite different,
but a similar element of discouragement may be found in both.

(5) The dying are those who are helped most by a well considered and carefully conducted ministry of prayer, especially
when the clergyman is spiritually poised in the situation. Death
and dying, in a unique sense, are the clergyman's department.
No one else speaks with any authority upon this experience.
The clergyman, both symbolically and orally, reminds his

[2] See *Comfort Ye My People*, p. 11.

parishioners of their beliefs which they may forget under the impact of the dying experience. Prayers with the dying must be carefully prepared so that they are positive in content.[3]

In ministering to non-parishioners one must be alert to the same five situations listed above but they must be checked against certain other observations which indicate prayer with non-church members. (1) If you are welcomed and accepted as a minister and not as a social companion; (2) if there is some expressed desire or need by the patient such as, "Remember me tomorrow," or "One has time to do a lot of thinking in a place like this"; (3) if some reference to religion is expressed such as, "My confidence is in my surgeon and God," or "I've been praying as best I could": then by all means have a prayer with the patient before you leave. These are all ways in which a non-parishioner asks for prayer even though he does not recognize what he has said himself.

The content of the prayer should be essentially the same as with a church member, for these persons who reach out for help may be thought of as members of the church invisible, children of God, and for all we know, they may have already gained places high in the Kingdom.

It is a privilege to stand beside people whose spirits are caught in the clasp of suffering and lift up those needs to God through prayer. It is for this task, perhaps even above others, that minister and member have been called; others may perform other tasks for us in time of need, but no one else is apt to perform this one.

[3] See *Comfort Ye My People*, pp. 39–73.

VIII

RECORDS

THE PASTOR HAS NOT KEPT RECORDS OF HIS PASTORAL WORK and personal counseling. This has been because of the confidential nature of his work, on the one hand, and his failure to understand the importance of records, on the other. The fact that he has not kept records is responsible, more than any other single thing, for the pastor's failure to develop a discipline equal to that of other professional workers in the humanitarian field. It is not enough to say he did not have the knowledge; if records had been kept the knowledge would have been forthcoming and the physician would now be turning to the clergyman for help instead of the amazing situation of the pastor turning to the physician for understanding of the spiritual problems of his own people. It is not that the physician disagrees with the pastor—he simply ignores him. It has not occurred to the physician that the pastor has much to contribute to the individual's welfare, either spiritually or physically. The great difference between the two professions is that the physician is studying his failures, keeping records of them, and publishing his observations, so that other members of the profession may learn from those failures, while the clergyman has all too often not even known when he has failed.

There are several types of pastoral records. One is the complete, detailed, verbatim record such as we have been using in our clinical training for ten years, as found in Chapter VI. This is a study record. It is written so that the minister may study it and examine the problems which were revealed during the call, but which he, and sometimes the parishioner, was not conscious of because of the emotional nature of the call, both because of the dynamic material dealt with and because of the extreme illness of the patient. Studying the record calmly, often studying two or three calls upon the same person at one time, the pastor may discover an underlying pattern of thought which he had not recognized previously.

Our progress and literature in the field of pastoral care will be based upon this type of record. It is interesting that such a record will reveal spiritual needs and faulty methods of which the pastor making the call and writing the records was not even conscious. It is through the use of such records that we will carry on our instruction, improve our effectiveness, and reclaim the pastoral task that is legitimately ours.

There is a second type of record which is a summary of a call with little or no direct quotation listed; here each call is recorded simply and new material is especially noted. This is a work record and is apt to reveal facts more than it reveals emotions, underlying problems, or the pastoral process. It is useful to the pastor largely in recalling topics which have been discussed with a given parishioner. It is not apt to reveal problems except as the pastor is conscious of them at the time of the conference. A pastor who is carrying a large burden of work, and who is skilled in recognizing emotions and emotional attitudes in relation to subjects discussed, will be able to use this type of record effectively. This record is not particularly useful for study purposes and contributes to knowledge only insofar as a large series of problems are studied in relation to a definite spiritual need.

The third type of record is simply a listing of the persons called upon or counseled with and the date of the contact, with no indication of what took place during the conference. This record is useful as a check upon himself by the pastor in his pastoral work. As yet we do not know what a work load is in pastoral calling or counseling. We know it varies from one person to another considerably, and we know that the number of calls made by some pastors is ridiculous. Little or no significant work can be done when one sees a different parishioner every few minutes. The hospital chaplain who makes thirty calls or more a day is doing ineffective work. Listing the number of one's calls sometimes reveals the type of work we are doing.

Another advantage of this type of record is that it keeps us from forgetting certain parishioners we would all like to forget. There are always a few such people in every parish. Dr. Henry Sloane Coffin has said, "The Lord will see to it that in every parish you will find a certain number of disagreeable people." If you "overlook" these persons when they are sick, or in your routine calling, you will not have helped your ministry nor your soul's confidence. A little attention sometimes does wonders for a paranoid person.

The careful minister will use all three of these types of records for he will have people with varying degrees of need.

PART THREE

THE PASTORAL TASK

IX

THE PASTOR GOES TO HIS PEOPLE

MANY PASTORS ASK, "HOW DO YOU GET PASTORAL COUNSEL-ing started?" By pastoral counseling they only visualize people coming to them for help. Others say, "No one ever comes to me for help." The tragedy of missed opportunities is contained in these words.

Pastoral work consists more in the pastor going to the people than it does in their coming to him, for the pastor who goes to his people ultimately will find them coming to him. In our study of human personality we have considered the abnormal in order to be able to recognize and understand the normal. We are now studying the normal, the commonplace, the usual. I used to assign my theological students' calls upon persons where there was known suffering; now I assign routine calls where no stress is known to be present when the call is made. It is surprising in what a large number of these calls stress is found.

As pastors we are interested in people first and problems second. Our point of view is: your problem is of no great concern to me aside from you and what it means to you, for I am not interested in which or how many of the commandments you have broken; I *am* interested in what the breaking of them means to you. In the same way I am interested in what you are facing and what you have been through in terms of your own spiritual condition.

With this thought in mind need we ask, "What are the opportunities for pastoral work? Is it necessary to get established in a church and become acquainted before you start your pastoral work?" It is not! The need for getting acquainted and established in a new church of itself presents an opportunity for pastoral work. To meet the official board, the teachers of the church school and the officers of the women's society formally at a reception is one thing but to go to them individually in their places of work and homes is quite another; to sit down and ask questions of them about their work, their families, their length of time in the church, their interests and hobbies is the essence of pastoral work when done properly.

The pastor should call first upon his official board, the officers of his women's society, his church school teachers and his young people's leaders upon starting his work in a new church. These are necessary administrative calls, but they also afford the opportunity for pastoral work and for laying the foundation for future work, for out of these calls will come information of special spiritual needs which may be followed up.

Upon coming to a new church the pastor should inquire of the President of the Board if he knows of any in the parish who are seriously ill or recently bereaved. He usually will not; it will be the president or some member of the women's society who will have this information, but the question will serve to impress upon the mind of the President of the Board that he should know, and that as lay leader of the congregation he has responsibilities beyond securing a preacher and balancing the budget.

If one is fortunate in following a pastor, and not a chore-boy, in a church, one's predecessor will have left a list of those who are seriously ill and recently bereaved, as well as those who are shut-in and aged, for the first two—the seriously ill and those who have lost loved ones within a year—should be called upon during the first week of one's ministry in a new church. This system works best in the Methodist Church where a minister leaves one week and another arrives the same week. In some denominations where the congregation does not realize their regular minister has gone for from three to six months there is little point to leaving a record of those who need special pastoral care other than the shut-ins and aged.

A. *The Dying*

The pastor's first responsibility is to the dying. For purposes of study I separate the sick and dying, for while the psychology of the sickroom of the person who is seriously ill and one who is not has many things in common, still we need to sharpen our conception of the pastoral task by having our ministry to the dying clearly in mind.

Many of our Protestant churches have largely given up their ministry to the dying. The reasons being those discussed in Chapter One; we have not felt we had anything especially to contribute. The fallacy of this belief has been demonstrated over and over again.[1]

In talking with a Lutheran pastor one day I asked, "For how many of your people are you called when they are dying?" He looked at me with something of wonder at the question. "Why, all of them," he said. "What happens when you are out of town?" I asked. He answered, "There is always someone to take the calls, either my assistant or a brother minister. I would no more think of not having my parish covered for emergency calls than a doctor would of going away without arranging for someone to take care of his patients."

Contrast this with a situation which came to my attention when a seriously ill patient in a Chicago hospital expressed the desire to see a minister of another denomination and it took three days to even find one, as all had gone off to a conference which had been called by one of the denominational leaders.

Ministry to the dying turns upon the relationship which has been built up through routine calling, through preaching and through whatever pastoral contacts one has had with a given

[1] See chapter VI; also, *The Art of Ministering to the Sick*, Cabot and Dicks, pp. 359–66.

person in the past, especially during the earlier phase of illness which precedes that leading up to the dying experience.

The emotional tone in the room of a dying person is apt to be quite tense so that a pastor, entering it, must have himself under emotional control if he is to make a positive contribution. He will be welcomed if his relationship is good with the family; if it is not then he will not even be admitted to the room and there is little that he can do about it. Above all he should not be overly insistent upon seeing a dying parishioner when he detects resistance by the family. If there are doubts about the wisdom of his seeing the patient, then he should give attention to the family as they will thus be reassured and helped by his understanding.

As a minister comes to know the physicians of his community, and as they see the effects of his work with their patients, they will welcome him to the sickroom as a co-worker and ally. The doctor is apprehensive toward the average clergyman because the training and thinking of the two are so different. Also, the doctor has seen many dying patients disturbed by overly-zealous clergymen, so he is apt to be protective of his patients. But as he sees tragedy disappear from a situation, and doubts and hostility turn into hope as the result of a minister's work, his attitude changes.

In this ministry the clergyman reminds the parishioner of what he may forget, under the impact of his suffering, not by what he says but by his presence. Through prayer, dormant spiritual resources are released which strengthen the parishioner. Dying is a lonely experience. Through prayer the parishioner is helped to realize he is not alone; that as he has known the companionship of God here, so he will know it more there; as he has been strengthened by loved ones here, so he will find loved ones there. Dying is a spiritual experience and the way one dies is a demonstration of faith and courage. At this point more than at any other the clergyman's own faith and quietness of spirit give strength. Especial care must be taken by the clergyman to conduct himself in a natural, friendly way. Our clergy have failed at this point frequently, so that the "funeral tone of voice" in clergymen is a description of a sentimental approach to death which all people of faith regret. The proper conduct in the presence of the dying is one of quiet, hopeful dignity and poise. Due deference should be paid the experience in which we are participating. Humor is out of place there as well as later in calling upon the bereaved.

The pastor's principal method in ministering to the dying is prayer. These prayers must be carefully prepared and attention must be given to making them positive in content.[2] As the dying process advances much of that which has interested the parishioner in the past becomes unimportant and unreal. His horizon closes down to one room, and then to a part of a room, until it includes only those who stand beside him, and finally only the voices of those who speak to him. When the pastor is working effectively the things of this world seem to give way to the realities of the next so that instead of death being a tragedy it becomes a triumph. This is what I call, "dying with enthusiasm." A mother who had caught a glimpse of the meaning of death following the death of a loved one, said, "We really weep because of our own loneliness and not because of any fears for him."

Effective ministry to the dying calls for time and persistency on the part of the pastor. During the last week of a person's illness, say with cancer, which is a disease that calls for much pastoral care, the minister may call every day and perhaps twice a day toward the end, each time having prayer but staying only a short time. Thus he is helpful both to the patient and to the family.

The pastor, above everything else, must be adaptable in this ministry. Because it has happened one way one time, or because

[2] See *Comfort Ye My People*, Dicks, Macmillan, pp. 37–73.

you read these lines, does not mean that it will happen that way each time. Anything may happen in the sickroom, and sooner or later it usually does.

B. *The Bereaved*

Bereavement is a personal crisis. It is characterized by loneliness. It matters not how strong one's belief in personal immortality may be, there is still the problem of separation which must be faced when a loved one dies. In bereavement the question of why a given person, particularly a child or young person, dies is raised frequently. There is seldom much question about the aged—the family say only, "We knew it would come but we were not ready."

Many of the questions and thoughts which arise in the minds of the bereaved have to do with things which are beyond the common mind, that is, they deal with God's justice, God's nature, and the nature of heaven. This is the clergyman's area of work and thinking.

The clergyman's ministry to the bereaved is limited by his parishioner's feelings toward him. If the pastor has failed in his ministry to the one who has died, particularly if that failure was due to his not calling during the illness, then his ministry to the family is apt to be ineffective. The minister who is disliked for any reason will not be helpful in this very intimate ministry regardless of his efforts. Thus, people often feel impelled to call another clergyman than their own minister in time of bereavement and they cannot understand a reluctance on the part of the one they call to respond to such a request. More people seem to be lost to the church because of the failure of the minister in bereavement than at any other time.

Another problem which crops up in bereavement, which many of our clergy overlook, is a feeling of guilt. This feeling may be justified through some failure on the part of the parishioner, or it may just be imagined; in either case it is real to the sufferer and must be dealt with if relief is to be gained. For example, a woman whose husband had been a rural mail carrier came to her minister with the request that he drive with her over her deceased husband's mail route. She said he had wanted her to go with him on this trip but she had always put it off. Now that he was dead she realized she would never be able to fulfill his request; such a desire had laid hold upon her to make the trip that she could not sleep. When she had asked her children to take her for the drive they laughed at her and told her she was foolish.

The minister should have taken the trip with her; it would have been a half day well spent. But that should not have ended his work with her. After their trip she needed to be helped to understand why she had had such a desire; perhaps there were other feelings of guilt and failure in their married life which needed pastoral attention.

Whenever excessive mourning, that holds over a long period of time, is observed it is well to explore for guilt feelings. This may call for time and effort on the pastor's part. If the bereaved is a young widow there is some risk of a transfer of affection to the minister. The pastor who is young and inexperienced and who is not especially happy with his own wife will do well not to attempt a full ministry to a bereaved young widow. She has time and the healing forces of nature on her side so that she will be able to work out of her bereavement with the aid of mild encouragement on the part of the minister. The pastor's wife should not enter into this task of ministry to the bereaved any more than she should other pastoral tasks.

Immediately upon receiving word of the death of a parishioner the pastor should call at the home unless there is some request to the contrary. The family will usually arrange for him to see an immediate member of the family; circumstances will vary somewhat. During the early moments of such a call events will determine the minister's actions and remarks; it is a matter of following leads. The intimacy of the pastor's acquaintance with the family and the deceased and the nature of the death will determine the few questions the pastor asks. This will be followed by a discussion of arrangements for the funeral. If there is the desire on the part of the family to have another pastor take part in the service the minister may offer to call the other pastor and make arrangements. This offer is usually welcomed eagerly, thus embarrassment for all is avoided.

A prayer with the family should follow. There are few exceptions to this rule. The purpose of this prayer is to commend the spirit of the loved one to God's care and to remind the bereaved of God's care of them, which they are apt to forget at such a time.[3]

In case the deceased is a non-parishioner and the pastor has a connection with him only through another member of the family, or where the community is small, the minister should call. He should follow the same general procedure as outlined above with the further specific statement to someone in the family, perhaps not the whole group, that he is willing to do anything possible to help, but that no obligations should be felt on the part of the family to ask him to have a part in the service. Of all acts that are unbecoming a clergyman, "corpse-chasing" is one of the greatest; at the same time this danger must not be permitted to block us out of performing our pastoral obligations to the bereaved.

The officiating clergyman may or may not go to the home immediately before the funeral. When he does he should have a prayer with the family before leaving for the church or funeral parlors. Following the formal funeral service the pastor should stay near the family until all have left the church or parlors, especially if the body is to be reviewed. The pastor, because he stands outside the family, can often help to quiet the already distraught feelings of the family by assisting those nearest the deceased. I ministered to a thirty-five-year-old

[3] See *Comfort Ye My People*, pp. 77–91.

woman through her final illness. The family was large and closely knit. One sister was especially close to the deceased girl. As the family came to the casket at the end of the funeral service this sister broke down and refused to move on. I stepped up beside her, stood a moment, then placed my arm around her and walked with her out of the church to the waiting car. She went for me, she would not have gone as readily for anyone else.

There is a trend away from the crude and non-Christian practice of viewing the body at the service, especially in the urban communities, just as there is a trend away from the practice of sentimental funeral sermons. The clergy can encourage this trend through conversation with the family. Some funeral directors recognize the desirability of keeping the casket closed during and after the service. Unfortunately many directors view their work as a business and not as an opportunity to be of service to suffering people; they believe their best advertisement is a well-displayed corpse which friends may admire, rather than a comforted family. We look toward the time when the non-Christian practice of worshipping dead bodies and cemeteries will have passed. The transition is slow, but there are some encouraging signs. More rapid progress could be made if clergy and funeral directors in given communities would sit down and discuss their mutual problems and practices in the light of the desire of both to be helpful to the bereaved. The clergyman can exert more influence upon funeral practices and consequently serve his people more effectively than he has done in most communities. Some pastoral associations have established committees to study this problem.

In planning a funeral service with a family Dr. Albert W. Palmer, formerly of Chicago Theological Seminary, has pointed out, "Remember it is their funeral, not yours." A family should be permitted to have anything it wants in the way of music, hymns, scriptural reading, poetry, sermon or sermons. The purpose of the funeral service is to bring comfort to the family;

it should not be considered an opportunity for a preacher to strike a blow at sinners he never sees except at such a time. There should be little basic difference in the service for a person who has committed suicide and the service for a faithful parishioner, for the most benevolent spirit or a poor beggar picked up beside the railroad track. The Christian message is a message of hope and it is our privilege to pronounce that hope at all times; it is best pronounced in the funeral service through selected scriptural passages and through prayer, although a carefully prepared statement which reminds the grief-stricken family of what they have forgotten may be of great help.

Important as the funeral service is, the pastor's greatest opportunity to minister to the bereaved comes after the funeral in the immediate days that lie ahead when loneliness lays its heavy hand upon them. Some pastors follow the custom of calling upon the bereaved once and then giving them no further care. This is a mistake. In one call the pastor cannot meet his obligation or fulfill his opportunity in ministering to the bereaved any more than one call upon a sick person is sufficient to meet the need there. Our pastoral work must be based upon the emotional need of the parishioner, not on the desires of the pastor. The clergyman who does not have time to minister effectively to the bereaved does not have time to do anything else, and the words he utters in his next sermon will be nauseating to God and a blasphemy to Christ.

The underlying conditions of a ministry to the bereaved are the same as in all our ministry—the suffering of the parishioner, the emotional relationship or rapport between parishioner and pastor, the stability, faith, and quiet confidence of the pastor in the face of suffering. Over and above that his ministry to the bereaved will turn upon his skill: his skill in following leads, and his skill in asking questions; his wisdom in not asking certain questions, and his ability in interpretation, the delicacy of his reassurance, and the spiritual resources tapped through his prayer. All of which adds up to the fine art of pastoral work.

C. *The Sick*

Through an increasing emphasis upon psychosomatic medicine the physician is coming to recognize the importance of the spiritual needs of his patients both as a cause of illness and as an aid to the recovery of health. The trend is toward the physician taking over this phase of the patient's care himself, however ineffective that care may be. If this trend continues as it has in the past ten years the clergyman's work will come under close scrutiny by the doctor. At present the average physician would like to bar ninety per cent of all clergymen from the sickroom; one cannot but be sympathetic with this desire in view of the lack of preparation by the clergyman for this most delicate of all delicate tasks. At the same time we know more now about the task of ministering to the sick than ever before; our clergy are becoming better trained for the pastoral task; and we are looking toward a day when we may join hands with the physicians in the care of the sick.[4]

Ministry to the sick and dying calls for the greatest skill of all pastoral work. With or without this skill, however, we are still welcome in the sickroom because the need there is so great. If we can just avoid doing harm we will be able to help ninety per cent of the people we call upon who are sick. A Boston surgeon lectured to my theological students upon the subject,

[4] *The Art of Ministering to the Sick,* Cabot and Dicks. The Macmillan Company, New York, 1936.

Religion and Health, Hiltner, chapter 2. The Macmillan Company, New York, 1943.

Religion in Illness and Health, Wise, chapter 2. Harper & Brothers, New York, 1942.

Who Is My Patient? Dicks. The Macmillan Company, 1942. For nurses, but contains significant new material for the clergyman; especially section on "Religious Needs of the Sick."

What Not To Do in the Sickroom. He went down the line with fifteen or twenty negatives: don't talk too much; don't stay too long; don't ask the patient what is wrong with him—if he wants you to know he will tell you; don't argue with the patient; don't tell him he is going to die; don't talk about someone else you know who had his disease and how long he was sick; don't force your prayer upon the patient; don't pray too long. A month later he stopped me in the hall to say, "In my lecture to the boys I overlooked the most serious mistake they will ever make in their work with the sick. I've just had two patients whose ministers made it. That is in failing to call at all upon their sick parishioners. That's one they'll never be forgiven."

Methods in ministering to the sick are the same as those used in other pastoral work and personal counseling which are discussed elsewhere, but there are certain major conditions in the sickroom in which more stress is present than in others, and these must be discussed here. While we should not distinguish between one parishioner and another so far as our efforts are concerned, it is certain that if our interest is in helping people and not primarily in making a good annual report, we will have to spend more time with one person than with another.

There are four situations in the sickroom which afford the clergyman his greatest pastoral opportunity. These are not exhaustive in that significant spiritual needs will not arise under other conditions in illness, but in these stress-situations lies the greatest opportunity for the pastor. He should call upon as many of his people who are sick as he can, but he should call more frequently and persistently upon persons going through the following experiences.

1. The surgical operation is a stress-situation, a personal crisis. From the surgeon's standpoint there are major and minor operations; from the patient's standpoint all are major—some are just more serious than others. The element of uncertainty and the dread of pain are present in every surgical patient. The

surgical operation is a spiritual experience, an experience of faith; faith in the surgeon, frequently an unknown person to the patient; faith in the nurses who are to care for the patient; faith in the hospital, its personnel and equipment; and faith in God working through nature to effect healing.

A Boston surgeon described the surgical operation as a religious rite. He said, "We have our high priests and acolytes, our ritual, incense and blood sacrifice." The acceptance of the religious rite by the god of surgical operations affects the patient more than any other person participating in the ritual. It is with faith that he goes into the ceremony, so he prepares himself before the operation, purging his conscience and examining his belief.

A patient in a Chicago hospital told me of having told a lie ten years before. Why did she feel the need to make this confession after ten years? Because the next morning she was facing a serious surgical operation during which she knew she might die. I had talked and prayed with her frequently but when she came seriously to prepare herself for the uncertain future, that lie stood out in bold relief against the background of the pending operation.

I used to ask pre-operative patients routinely the question, "How do you feel about it?" The great majority answered, "My faith is in my surgeon and God." The surgeon was thought of before God but then he had been punching them around recently in his examination and was more real to them. Perhaps they were right anyway, in thinking first of the importance of the surgeon, for a surgeon can ruin God's efforts, while we know God will not spoil a surgeon's work.

Since the surgical operation is a religious experience, an experience of faith, a parishioner will need any help the pastor can give him. In my early work as a hospital chaplain practically all of the requests which came from patients themselves for my services were from pre-operative patients. As one girl, facing an operation for cancer of the lung, put it, "I know the surgeon can do only so much and that the patient must do the rest. I was afraid I wouldn't be able to do my part so I wanted to see a minister." She was right in her reasoning. A minister ought to be able to help her at that time. I think I did; I know I did later as she approached death.[5]

The time to see a parishioner who is facing surgical treatment is the night before the operation. There are several reasons for this choice, the primary one being that through the pastor's reassurance the patient may be helped to relax and thus secure a good night's sleep, which is needed. To be sure, most physicians give a sleeping potion, but even a drug is aided in its work by the patient's cooperation. Another reason for calling the night before is that the pre-operative routine of the hospital is avoided. Surgeons like to start their work quite early which means the patient is prepared even earlier. The result is that although the clergyman may arrive at the hospital by seven or eight o'clock he invariably interrupts the pre-operative preparations.

The minister should, whenever possible, be present during the operation, sometimes going into the anaesthetic room with the patient, then returning to the family to be with them during the long wait. Some ministers like to be present to watch surgery. I have done this frequently; more experience has led me to believe the pastor's place is with the family once the patient is asleep.

2. The second major stress-situation we see in illness is in the person facing life with a physical handicap following his illness. Loss of eyesight, loss of hearing, loss of a limb or limbs, inability to walk through an injury to one's spine, joints stiffened by arthritis, restricted activity following a heart attack, diabetes which necessitates the regular taking of medication, the colostomy treatment for cancer of the rectum, which may involve radical and disfiguring surgery; these and others are con-

[5] *The Art of Ministering to the Sick*, p. 359.

ditions calling for heightened courage and adjustment on the part of the patient.

The mental workings of a person facing life with a handicap are complicated. At that time especially he is thrown back upon his basic beliefs, his faith. To injure one's body is to injure one's soul, for an injured body means a hurt spirit and broken pride. "This has happened to me," we think, "to me of all the people I know." Then we ask the question. "Why? Why has my world, my God singled me out?" Most of us can find reasons for what has happened to us, even though our conclusions are actually quite unfounded. For instance, a guilt feeling is more apt to be present in a person facing life with a handicap than in a dying person. It is little comfort to point out to a handicapped person how many others have the same condition; in fact, it may do harm unless the physician or clergyman doing so has the complete confidence and affection of the patient.

Since the facing of a handicap is a spiritual experience, as is the facing of an operation, here again is a need and an opportunity for the clergyman. Not always will a patient want to talk about this problem with his clergyman but he should be given the opportunity to if he wishes. Sometimes he will be helped most by being treated perfectly naturally by the pastor; this is especially true if there is a feeling of guilt present. It may be weeks, months, even years before a person can talk about his attitude to his pastor and then it may be quite a different attitude from the one he had at the onset of his handicap. Take plenty of time, be natural and easy, but give many opportunities for the patient to talk about himself if he wants to. As God's representative you are willing to face anything your parishioner wants to talk about. In that way you demonstrate God's affection to the suffering person.

Above all, handicapped persons do not want a sickly, sentimental sympathy. They want to think of themselves as natural, normal, healthy people. If they are treated otherwise they withdraw and become depressed. A woman who had a tracheotomy tube in her throat told me of hearing one of a group of school children say to the others as they passed her home, "The woman who lives there has a tube in her throat!" Imagine the heightened feeling of isolation which followed!

A man of thirty-five became paralyzed as a numbness in his feet crept up his legs and into his hands. Then for some months his disease did not progress, but he was confined to his chair and bed. He reviewed his whole situation—his future, his family, his financial resources and what his handicap would mean to his attractive young wife and two children. He concluded that the insurance money would educate the children and after a time his wife would probably remarry, so he planned to commit suicide. Before he could carry out his plan the disease began to advance. Eventually he found his way to our hospital and it was there I got to know him. He was a talented musician and a brilliant conversationalist. During his first hospitalization we spent hours together talking of many things but not of his plan to commit suicide, his lost music or his inability to work. It was months later that we reached the place in our relationship where we could talk about his suicidal plan and his future.

Another person with a terrific handicap asked me quite seriously to help her plan her suicide as there was no reason for her continuing to live. All she had to do was to stop taking an expensive drug for a few days and the job would have been done, but she seemed not to have thought of that and I did not feel inspired to point out anything so obvious. She never committed suicide, but I think she seriously desired to.

The first days when a parishioner is facing a handicap are important ones for the clergyman and he will do well to call frequently and in a leisurely way. To face a handicap is to feel alone, deserted by God and isolated from friends. The pastor can do much toward overcoming both these feelings, and in preventing the family from over-protecting him. A handicapped person's greatest problem is with those surrounding him who try to protect him. This is a serious mistake.[6]

3. The long convalescence is another stress-situation found in illness. For some barren spirits anything after two days is a long convalescence, while for others the crisis of time does not set in for weeks. There are a number of diseases which call for long confinement to bed, to a wheel chair, to hours where activity is limited and the sufferer is dependent upon those around him. After a while he tires of reading and his imagination runs bare, then loneliness and boredom possess his spirit like devils dragging a soul to hell. When he has passed the physical crises and is moving slowly up the long road toward recovery the physician turns to more acute problems, the nurses are dismissed, families go about their tasks, and his friends accept the fact that he is out of the picture; they may call, but, having been once, they go on about their own affairs. Then he comes to the conclusion that no one really cares, after all, and he sees that the world can go on without his help.

The clergyman's ministry is important during acute illness and he must not neglect it, but his greatest opportunity in ministry to the sick is with the person going through a long convalescence. His first call during the early days of an illness is taken for granted—everyone calls then; in fact too many call. His second call is hardly expected but is accepted with appreciation. "Great fellow, that minister," says the patient, "he really gets around." Boredom is beginning to set in so that when the pastor calls a third time he is greeted like a long-lost friend; the fourth and fifth and sixth calls follow and instead of "parishioner-minister" it now becomes "Fred and Joe." Family and friends are astonished at an interest and devotion to religion that seems to have started with father's illness. I repeat, the minister's greatest opportunity is with the long convalescent.

[6] *Greet the Man*, Wilke, Christian Education Press, Philadelphia.

4. Those facing death present the fourth major crisis of illness. While it is impossible to separate the ill from the dying or to be able to describe one's work as ministering to the sick at one point and to the dying at another, I have separated them for purposes of description and to sharpen our understanding of the pastoral task.

D. *The Hospital Call*

Both ministers and laymen have occasion to call upon parishioners and friends who are patients in hospitals. Because of the increasingly complicated institution which the hospital is and because of the involved nature of illness, most persons who make such calls feel apprehensive lest they do or say something which will do harm to the patient and delay his recovery. Some who do not feel such apprehension would do better if they did, for it is the gabby, over-confident person, who "has had an operation" himself that does most harm. And do not think it is hard to do harm in the sickroom. It is very easy. In fact I have known patients—not many, but more than one—who were killed by well-meaning callers who came in the name of religion, but lacked understanding of the emotional nature of illness. Their conception of ministry to the sick was to prepare the patient to meet his maker through converting him to their religious beliefs.

It is easy to do harm in the sickroom, very easy. A kind-hearted member of the hospital board where I was formerly a chaplain used to call throughout the hospital. Time after time I came across patients whom he had annoyed because he was tedious in his inane conversation. Yet because he was a member of the hospital board no one did anything about his calling.

The sickroom is one of the most highly emotionally charged situations, particularly the hospital sickroom, into which we enter. This is because illness centers the sick person's attention upon himself, through pain and fever and the strangeness of the hospital routine. His clothes are taken away from him, he is taken care of by young women who have a curious disregard for one's privacy, and he is required to submit to all kinds of strange, and often painful, tests and examinations. Beyond that there is the uncertainty of the outcome of the illness, even though it is a comparatively mild one. Into this situation and under these conditions the minister and the friend is expected to enter and not only avoid hurting the patient still more but actually to make a positive contribution to his spiritual and physical well-being.

Let me describe the specific steps one needs to follow in making a call upon the sick so as to avoid doing harm, for if one can avoid hurting a patient through calling at the wrong time, staying too long or too short a time, through talking too much or about the wrong subjects, through sitting down when one should stand up or standing up when one should sit down, through kicking the bed or leaning upon it, through praying too long or too loudly or through failing to pray at all, and finally, through failing to know how to leave the sickroom— if all these can be avoided—then God will use you to the patient's benefit.

The first step in making a hospital call is to get to the patient. The proper procedure is to go to the information desk and inquire where the patient is. If you are a minister you will be permitted to call out of visiting hours. The reason for this is that the hospital authorities recognize that the minister can be of most help to the patient when there are no visitors present; also that he is a busy person. The only exception to calling out of visiting hours is upon obstetrical patients: here no one is permitted in the room while the baby is with the mother. The pastor would do well to find out at what hours the babies are with the mothers, write this information upon a card so that he always has it, and make his calls accordingly. The ideal time for the minister's call in the hospital is between ten and eleven-thirty in the morning; this gives the nurses time to have completed the morning routine of bed pans, baths, making the beds, and other general care. The doctor will have made his rounds and the family and visitors will not have arrived.

A word should be said about calling in semi-private, or two-bed, rooms. Here tremendous harm is done through the indifference of visitors. The caller should observe the condition of the other patient upon entering a room. If he is sleeping, or if he obviously is quite sick, make your call very brief. Above all, do not feel obligated to speak to the other patient unless you are introduced by the person you are calling upon and unless the other patient is responsive and shows an interest in you. Your responsibility is to your own parishioner. You need to be considerate of the other patient even when your parishioner insists that you stay longer or talks in a loud voice himself.

Upon going to the information desk to inquire about a parishioner place your card upon the desk in front of the girl and say, "I am Reverend Mr. Blank. I believe you have Mrs. Smith, who is one of my parishioners." The girl will both hear and see by your card that you are a minister. If for any reason she fails to give you a pass or information as to where your parishioner is, do not argue with her; or if later the nurse denies you admission to your parishioner's room do not argue with her. Call the family to see if they know of any reason you should not call; if they know of none—call the doctor in charge, and then go to the administrator of the hospital. He is the one who makes the rules and only he can change them.

Once you are on the floor where your patient is, go to the nursing desk and inquire if it is all right to see Mrs. Smith. If the nurse is alert and has sufficient time she will accompany you, or will ask an assistant to, to see if Mrs. Smith is prepared to see a caller. It is not helpful to start a call by embarrassing your parishioner in case she is enthroned upon a bed pan or if she is not properly covered. If the nurse hesitates about your calling, then inquire how Mrs. Smith is, if she is resting, or if this is a bad time to call. If Mrs. Smith has not slept for three nights and has just been given a hypo the nurse may be debating whether your call will be of more help than the drug, and she is right in considering such a question. If the doctor has left strict orders that no one is to call, then you will need to call him to inquire if you can be of help. The doctor is responsible for the patient's total welfare, including his spiritual and emotional condition. Some take this responsibility seriously and recognize the minister as an ally; some do not. Some have had bad experiences with ministers and are on the defensive toward them. In that case you can report to the family that you have called and will be glad to call again if they will let you know when the patient is able to see you. Do not argue with the nurse or doctor about whether you should or should not see a person. You may be absolutely right but they are doing the best they can, ignorant though they may be, and your disagreeing with them only gains their ill will and does not change their opinions.

Once in the room you follow the leads that the patient gives you, for your task is to serve him, not to force your own ideas upon him, or to tell him stories of your own experiences as a patient. He is his own spiritual physician—you are the medicine. *If given the chance he will carry you to his spiritual need.* Both minister and friend deal with the spiritual side of the patient's need whether it is through laughter or prayer. If he puts out his hand to you—take it, but do not give it that old one-two handshake. Govern the vigor of your handclasp by his. If he asks you to sit down, do so. If he talks about the weather, the flowers on his table, the church, his doctor, his operation, death, the nurse, his work, his wife, or his pain, let him talk.

If he weeps, swears, prays, do not be surprised and do not argue. Be pleasant but not disgustingly cheerful; be concerned but not sticky and sentimental. When he shows some sign of restlessness, or if he is only mildly responsive, ask a couple of questions, express your interest in him and then leave. That will impress him. But come back again and observe the difference in the way he receives you. If he expresses an interest in the church, or religion, or is appreciative of your call, have prayer with him. Choose your words well but make the prayer brief. The length of the twenty-third psalm is about the proper length of a prayer in the sickroom. The content of your prayer should be hopeful and reassuring.[7] When you are ready to leave—go to the door, say good-bye, and leave. It is that simple, but some make a difficult job of it.

Remember that our Lord said, "When I was sick ye visited me—inasmuch as ye did it unto the least of these, my brethren, ye did it unto me." In calling upon the sick you are serving Him as you serve the patient and friend.

E. *Special Needs*

A special need that must be listed high in our scale of pastoral opportunities centers in the family where there is unemployment on the part of the breadwinner. This problem usually brings the parishioner to the pastor, but there are many times when the pastor must be the aggressor, due to embarrassment and hesitancy on the part of the family. Information concerning such a situation may reach the pastor through another parishioner or through a social worker. During the depression social workers often called the pastor of a family where there was a moral problem due to apprehension brought about by unemployment; more might have been called had those first clergymen succeeded in their task. We confidently believe that as the social worker and clergyman learn to work together in the future the pastor will be one of the first to be called by the social worker as problems arise concerning parishioners. See Chapter XIII for further discussion of this problem.

Occasionally, even in the best of churches, parishioners go to jail. A young minister told me the story of one of his boys in the Young People's Department being put in jail because of

---

[7] See *Comfort Ye My People*, Dicks, Macmillan Company, for Scriptural readings and prayers for the sickroom.

a serious automobile accident for which he was responsible. The pastor sent the boy word that he was "behind" him, but did not call at the jail lest his parishioners think he was taking the boy's part. We can imagine that the boy felt his pastor was so far "behind" him that it made no difference.

Most judges consider a pastor's interest a vital factor in determining the disposal of a problem which comes before them. The pastor needs to be intelligent in appealing to a judge and should remember that the judge has studied the problem and may know more than he does about the proper disposition of a charge. At the same time every judge knows that membership in a church where the minister is interested in his people is a stabilizing and constructive force in an individual's life.

F. *The Aged and Shut-Ins*

The aged and shut-ins are the most commonly neglected persons in our parishes; we take them for granted and day after day postpone our calls upon them. When we do call there seems to be little spiritual need present. Their conversation is repetitive as their lives are reasonably uneventful, and we are led to believe there are no spiritual needs. We take their expressions of appreciation and their delight in our attention to them as flattering to ourselves instead of being an indication of their great loneliness. There is another reason, more definite, less flattering which constitutes the real reason why we postpone our calls upon these persons. Because of their condition they seem unlikely to make much contribution to the ongoing program of the church. There are many demands upon the pastor's time, still we know that the clergyman, like everyone else, does what he wants to do. We may conclude, therefore, that there is only one sound reason for the pastor's neglecting the aged and shut-ins—that is because he does not want to call upon them. All other reasons are just plain poppycock. In the making of these calls the true pastor's heart is tested, for the only reward from calling on this group is a spiritual reward. It is possible to test a clergyman's spiritual depth by inquiring if he calls upon his aged and shut-in persons.

The aged may be shut-in in that they cannot leave their homes, their rooms, their beds, or they may be able to go out for walks and do a few things about the home or farm. It calls for real imagination to keep an elderly person occupied and happy, and this task is not primarily the pastor's. At the same time, since his is the spiritual oversight of his people, he will be the one who will discover a miserable older person whose family is concerned only with his physical wellbeing and who have overlooked or ignored his loneliness. They often cannot understand why he is grouchy and unpleasant. The pastor may make suggestions as to how time and mind may be filled more interestingly so as to overcome that feeling of being unneeded and unwanted. He contributes to its relief insofar as he breaks the loneliness but he contributes more than the average person does in calling because he personalizes the faith that sustains an older person in the evening hours of life. He represents, in a unique way, the life which is still ahead. Increasingly, as the aged person's friends cross over to the other life, as his body's strength drops away, as his thoughts turn to the life before him, he will want and need the encouragement of his pastor. Thus, while the minister in his calls will listen to the parishioner's recital of his day's events, small and of little consequence to the pastor but of great importance to the parishioner, he will also listen to the repeated recital of past experiences, and he must not fail to bring the comfort and reassurance of faith which is gained through prayer. It will be through the pastor's faith and through his Bible reading, prayer and the communion service, that this ministry of reconciliation will be carried on.

Many have noted the tendency of an aged person to live in the past and to speak of the past as the years move on. This is an easily understood tendency, for with the slowing up of the physical strength the mind reverts to the past and dwells

upon the years of action. With the passing of time the stories
often change also. Bishop Francis A. McConnell tells the story
of an old uncle of his who was fond of reminiscing of his Civil
War experiences. One particular story was told repeatedly
and, as the years passed, it took on more and more glamour. In
its original form the story was simply that Bishop McConnell's
uncle had been sent out to search for food. He approached a
smokehouse behind the Southern picket lines, but before the
lock on the door could be forced a Southern patrol fired on him.
However, he made his way back to his own lines and to safety.
It was in this form that Bishop McConnell first remembered
the story. But with the passing years first one man was killed
and then another until the whole Southern patrol fell at the
hand of the soldier. One day the Bishop said to the old man,
"Uncle, I remember that story as you told it years ago. No one
was killed in the story then. You were only fired on but es-
caped." The old man looked him over carefully then said with
finality, "Frank, as I have grown older I find that my memory
has grown better!"

These stories which the aged tell are not in themselves important. What is important is the emotional and spiritual satisfaction, the feeling of friendliness, which accompanies the telling. If loneliness is the major problem of the aged, and if loneliness is a sense of isolation, then the pastor has an important
role to perform in preventing that sense of isolation from becoming too complete and absolute.

Many churches are establishing clubs and programs especially for older people. The Methodist Church has experimented
with conferences for older people. With the steadily mounting
age level, and with more and more people living beyond the age
of sixty-five, the church must give more attention to this
group. A vitally important study of the churches' ministry to
older people has been conducted by the Federal Council of
Churches Department of Pastoral Services under the direction
of the Reverend Seward Hiltner. Lennert Cedarleaf and Paul

Maves, who conducted the study, are both clinically trained, alert young clergyman. This study represents a new outreach of the church in its ministry to individuals.[8]

Shut-ins may be elderly or they may be young or middle-aged persons who have had some physical handicap which limits their physical activity. This condition often does not limit their mental and spiritual activity, but it frequently is permitted to. Occupational therapy works in this field and will become increasingly important in the future. Occupational therapy grew largely out of World War I; following World War II it took great strides forward in its work with veterans. A few communities, especially in New England, have employed therapists on a county and state basis who give attention to the rehabilitation of the physically handicapped. It is to be hoped that this practice will become general. The minister is in a position to aid in the establishing of such a service in his community.

The clergyman should be informed as to what resources of this nature are available. Such information can be gained through the local family welfare society. When there is no trained personnel available to carry on work both of diversion and rehabilitation with the shut-ins, the clergyman may have to assume some responsibility in helping a parishioner make plans for the use of his time. A young man of thirty-three, who could not walk, needed encouragement to undertake a plan of selling stationery, Christmas cards and magazines. His improvement, mentally and spiritually, was marked from the day his plan got under way. Another man I knew had been handicapped seven years, being unable to leave his wheel chair, yet he was busy writing radio script. Another, a man who had lost both his legs, lived alone with his dog, doing all his own housework and cooking. He took great delight in training his dog to run errands and to do numerous tricks.

The problems of the handicapped are tremendous ones and the chief one is the isolation of loneliness. Newspapers, maga-

[8] *The Church and Older People*, Maves and Cedarleaf.

zines and books, and the radio keep them in touch with the outside world and afford them entertainment. The radio especially
makes a great contribution to the shut-in, but it is not enough.
It is all in-going; for development, spiritually and mentally,
there must be some out-going thought and activity. Attention
must be given to the fellowship which comes through belonging to the church visible. Visits by members of the church to
the shut-ins can be planned and communion should be taken
to them regularly.

G. *Evangelistic Calling*

Most persons will affiliate with the church only after contact
with the pastor and many only after receiving instruction. We
hope that the day is fast approaching when the practice of receiving uninstructed persons into full membership of the
church will be a thing of the past. There are still many situations, however, when the invitation to membership is given
and persons who are unknown to the pastor will respond. This
practice represents the weakness of the Protestant Church and
should not be encouraged. Still it is done. In many situations it
is possible to come into the church knowing little of its teaching or history, and understanding little of its spiritual resources
or practices. Unfortunately many seem to learn little after
they join.

The church must constantly be alert to the ever-present task
of enlisting new members. The days of mass evangelism are
passing. New methods must be substituted for the old.

Pastoral calling as a method of evangelism is not new. Our
Lord spoke to certain ones saying, "Follow me." His followers
have used that method through the generations by singling out
certain individuals and saying, "I want you for Christ." Sometimes they have been successful and sometimes they have not,
depending upon accompanying circumstances.

In their calling upon prospective members some pastors have

thought that if they could out-talk the prospect he would be won. This out-talking often leads to arguing. The best way to convince a person he is right in an idea he holds is to argue with him that he is wrong. Any evangelistic effort which is based upon talking a person into the church is doomed to failure; you cannot argue people into the kingdom of heaven, any more than you can shout them in.

Our Lord used the method of love. The early church was founded upon fellowship; whenever it has forgotten that it has failed. We see organized religion popular wherever the church is founded upon fellowship, regardless of the theology it teaches. Perhaps love is what religious people have in common, after all.

Pastoral work, as I am describing it, is founded upon love.[9] The pastor's method in calling upon prospective members is the same as it is upon his parishioners. He does not need to tell people why he calls unless it is to reassure them concerning his interest in them; they know that he is a clergyman and as such is interested in their spiritual welfare. To bring the subject of church membership to their attention and to bring them hurriedly to a decision concerning their spiritual condition is like proposing to a young lady upon first acquaintance.

There are many people who have been reared in families where there is little or no love between mother and father, consequently there was little sound affection for their youngsters. These persons, as they become adults, will be suspicious of affection and will have little comprehension of the fellowship of the church in Christ; the grace of God will be beyond their understanding. They often succeed in marrying fine young men and women only to lead their husbands and wives a miserable life because, basically, they are miserable themselves. They lack security at the point where they should feel most secure; they do not know how to love or be loved. The pastor, calling upon such persons, faces the difficult task of demon-

[9] See chapter III.

strating God's interest in them and this can best be done through his own affection for them.

The main purpose of the call upon the prospective member is to express an interest in the person and to overcome any hesitancy which may be felt on the prospect's part toward the church. Such a call should offer the opportunity to ask any questions concerning the beliefs and practices of the church which may be in the prospect's mind. If there are children in the home who are in the church school they will be a subject of conversation. Many parents will come to church with their children when an interest is taken in them by the pastor.

It has been reported that of the converts made by the Roman Catholic Church, many first became interested through care received in some hospital run by Roman Catholics. This proves that when a person is in difficulty and receives help he is impressed by those who help him. Love begets love; interest begets interest. Illness and suffering should not be taken advantage of for purposes of evangelism; at the same time we know that suffering opens doors for pastoral care, and out of pastoral care arises the desire for continued fellowship in the church. A man who had been sick for some time and upon whom we had called regularly for ten months sent for me one day. He said, "You fellows have been so decent to me. I'd like to get on your books. I'd like to join your church. How do I go about it?" He did not need to be told why we had called upon him. He knew that as individuals we would not have even known of his illness had we not been ministers.

Calling upon prospective members is a matter of establishing a satisfactory and reassuring relationship, a matter of listening, of taking time. There will be a response when there is a need on the part of the prospect; when there is no need present any amount of persistence and argument will be to no avail.

Transferring a personal loyalty to the larger loyalty of Christ and God and the church is one of the most delicate tasks we face as pastors, and one in which we commonly fail. This fact is more generally true among the free church denominations than among the liturgical denominations. One Sunday morning I was told by a member of the official board of a large church in a Southern city that people had come as far as "twenty miles" that morning just to hear Dr. Blank preach because of their affection for him; there was no mention of their love for the church into which he had brought them. Such a statement indicates the limitations of that pastor's ministry, yet his board and his brethren would think of him as one of the most effective ministers in that whole area.

Two or three things can be said conclusively upon this problem. First, in those churches where preaching is emphasized, this problem is more acute than in traditions where preaching is not prominent, such as the Roman Catholic and the Episcopal churches, especially the Anglo-Catholic wing. I have often heard members of one of these churches express criticism of their clergy, yet their loyalty to the church never wavered. In some of our Protestant churches if the members do not like the clergyman they absent themselves from the church and may never return. As Protestants we have claimed "the message" characterizes our tradition, therefore the pulpit has been placed in the center of the church. The trend now is to place the cross and the altar in the center of the church and the pulpit at the side. Symbolically this is a great step forward.

Secondly, more careful instruction of our people before they are received into the church should help to overcome this problem of transferring the personal loyalty to the larger loyalty. This involves instruction in the history of the church, its sacraments, symbols and practices, and an actual follow-up to be certain that those who need it are oriented in the fellowship of the church.

In light of my contention that loneliness is the great emotional problem of our time, the strengthening of the spirit of fellowship is one of the greatest evangelistic attractions the church has; at the same time this fellowship must be God-centered or it deteriorates into a club or an association of persons of goodwill.

H. *The Routine Call*

There seems to be no adequate term to describe the average everyday call which is made upon parishioners regardless of their spiritual needs and without specific purpose in the way of church organizational promotion. For want of a better term I have called them routine calls. This call is made for no other reason and with no other excuse than that a given person is a member of a given church. In some respects this is the most effective and most appreciated call the pastor makes because he calls of his own volition; not because someone is sick or bereaved, and not to promote some program or make some request. This is the kind of calling upon which the church of another generation was founded. When older parishioners bemoan the passing of "the good old days" in the church or when they speak of "the grand old pastors," it is this type of call that they are talking about. Just how much of it was done in "the good old days" is difficult to ascertain because reminiscences of the past have a tendency to take on an exaggerated glamour. Whether our fathers in the faith actually succeeded in carrying on such work extensively or not is unimportant; that they did more than we are doing we may be sure. Such calls are the heart of pastoral work, the foundation stones, the mother and father, the essence, the alpha and omega, all wrapped into one.

The routine call serves two purposes: it builds up the relationship between pastor, people and God, and it puts the pastor in a position to discover spiritual and emotional needs in an incipient stage before they have become serious problems.

As we have seen in Chapter III, the emotional relationship between pastor, parishioner and God is one of the underlying conditions that make for effective pastoral work. Without this satisfying feeling of friendliness the pastor does harm when the parishioner is suffering. To establish this feeling is difficult or impossible unless the parishioner believes you are interested in him, and unless he believes the pastor is interested he is not apt to think that God is. The most common rebuke faced by the officers of the church when soliciting funds is that "the church is not interested in me." By the church is usually meant "the minister," although when laymen call upon other members in the name of the church the failure of the pastor is overlooked. In one respect no other caller can take the place of the pastor, for he represents the church and God in a unique sense.

We are often impatient with parishioners who assume the attitude, "The church is not interested in me"; we think and sometimes say, "Are you interested in the church?" This is an unfair attitude. The church is a fellowship. The Christian movement grew out of the experience of a little group of people collected around Jesus who had sought them out saying, "Follow me." He was the aggressor. It was much later, after months and years of teaching, working and living together that "the message" or "gospel" of Jesus came to mean much to them. In fact it seems to have been only after Jesus had died and risen from the dead that they became an ongoing fellowship who were interested in proclaiming his "gospel" and even then they were such a loosely knit, quarreling, strong-headed lot that Jesus had to give them leadership of a strong and personal nature for a long time. Then only a few seemed to grasp the meaning of His message; most of them were concerned with His life and personality. Perhaps we should remember the slowness of those early Christians in grasping his message when we become impatient with the church. It was not Christ's message but His personality that caught their loyalty and held it. It was His pastoral touch, His personal interest in them that attracted and held them. That is the basis upon which rapport is founded. It is also the essence of pastoral work.

The second significant reason for the routine call is that the pastor is able to discover incipient needs before they become serious beyond the point of remedy. The physician is always bemoaning the fact that patients delay seeing a doctor when a suspicious lump, pain or lesion does not heal. When months later a physician's help is sought he discovers that a cancer which could have been taken care of easily when it was first noticed by the patient is now past surgical treatment. The same thing is true in the spiritual field. With so many of our people unhappily married, many of whose problems could be overcome through counseling, we need to be constantly alert for difficulties. Most of our counseling in the marital field, especially at the outset of our work with a given family, will start with the wife. Therefore calling in the home, if the pastor is alert and skillful, will uncover some of these difficulties before the marriage is seriously threatened. In its various phases the pressures of human suffering, especially apprehension, will come easily to the pastor's attention when he is available and has the spiritual welfare of his people at heart, as contrasted with the all-too-common clergyman who is concerned with the church program but forgets the people.

The pastor is not an expert in all the problems he comes across, neither is the general physician in his field, neither is the public health nurse, neither is the teacher. But the pastor, like the doctor, knows that a great percentage of the problems he faces will straighten out with a little help and encouragement. We recognize that without that help and encouragement, small as it may seem, many will develop into serious, perhaps irreparable trouble. There are probably ten per cent who cannot be helped at all, regardless of who tries, then there are another ten per cent, as a rough guess, who need help, expert help, and it becomes the pastor's responsibility to get them to someone who can supply it. In many instances he will be able to cooperate in the treatment.

If the pastor waits for these needs to come to him, few of them will ever come. He finds them; his help is accepted because he has demonstrated his interest in his people by actually going to them. It is more than talk, it is a demonstration. There are many consecrated clergymen who have excellent ideas about church promotion who are literally working themselves to death with promotion work; their sermons are well thought out and effectively delivered; yet their ministries are failing. Their people have gotten the idea the pastor is not interested in them and they are right. He is interested in Christ, he is interested in bringing people to God, he is interested in welfare work for the poor. He is *not* interested in his own parishioners. If someone comes to him for help he will work his heart out; his parishioners know that, but still they feel cool toward him. One thing he fails to do: *he does not ring door bells;* he does not go to the people!

X

THE PEOPLE COME TO THE PASTOR

A. *Pre-Marital Counseling*

FOREMOST AMONG COUNSELING PROBLEMS WHICH COME TO the pastor are those couples who desire to be married. To be sure, they seek the pastor's help for the ceremony of marriage, with little thought of more than a conference about the ritual itself. To go further into a discussion of some of the factors that make for a successful marriage calls for tact and judgment, but our people are so poorly prepared for marriage that some pastors feel the clergy must assume major responsibility in the field if the church is not to fail its people in the area of the home.

Marriage may be considered successful when the affiliation contributes positively to the personalities of the two parties, thus enabling them to make their own contribution in the wise and affectionate rearing of their children. As a conservative estimate it is safe to say that only about ten to twenty per cent of our people are happily married; that does not mean that all the others are complete failures. This high degree of failure in marriage reveals that something is seriously wrong so far as our marriage practices are concerned. A regime of suppression, moralism and preachments will make no contribution to this problem. We have had that. The alternative of education, enlightenment and understanding holds some hope. At least it has not been tried.

The clergyman is in a strategic position in relation to the

marriage problem and many are carrying on counseling in the field. Ideally the pastor should discuss the emotional and spiritual forces which go to make up a successful marriage and refer the couple to a physician for information upon family planning and the art of sexual happiness. Many pastors, particularly the younger clergy, serving in small communities, will not have a physician in the community who is well enough informed to carry his part of this counseling problem. Rather than trying to carry the whole load himself the pastor should contact a physician in a larger town who is capable of doing this work. Such a contact can be made through a pastor friend who will know the physicians in his community. In normal times a drive of a hundred miles or farther is not unreasonable for such counsel.

Secondly, where there is no doctor who is equipped to work in the field of birth control and sex education, the pastor may cultivate such an interest in his doctors and urge them to assist in this type of counseling. Some physicians will be reluctant, especially where there is considerable public opinion against the spreading of family planning information, but when the pastor refers couples to the physician for examination and counsel most doctors will cooperate. No girl should be married without an examination, for many a distressing experience and ultimate shipwreck of a home may be avoided by a few simple suggestions. The pastor cannot urge such an examination too strongly.

Further, the pastor may put certain literature into the couple's hands when they come seeking his services for marriage. There are many books available. Some may be loaned, others given outright. Some ministers give Foster Wood's little book, "*Harmony in Marriage*," to every couple they marry.[1]

---

[1] Federal Council of Churches, New York, $1.00.

Marriage and Sexual Harmony, Butterfield, Emerson Books, New York, $.50, is even better on the physical side of marriage.

Pre-marital counseling should include a consideration of the couple's plans for their own home. If they plan to live with parents the pastor may question this decision. While such a question may be considered none of his business, still his interest will be appreciated. No healthy, normal couple will want to live with their in-laws, but for some reason such may be the plan. The pastor's suggestions to the contrary may be sufficient to influence them to make another decision. I would not be insistent upon this point unless there was some real question already in the minds of the couple.

The pastor is called upon to marry many persons who are not members of his church and here the question should be raised about what plans they are making for a church home. The couple may not do anything about it at the time but the thought will have been planted in their minds. Five or six years later concern for their own youngster may bring them to church. At the time when a couple is making their plans for their lives together they are most receptive and appreciative of a pastor discussing their plans for a church home together also. In fact to fail to do so is to show indifference toward them.

As clergymen we should make an effort to follow up the couples we have married. This may be done through a personal call periodically and especially upon or near the date of their anniversary, or through a letter. Too often we have married our young people, pocketed our fee and gone merrily on our way, accepting no further responsibility and failing to see a further opportunity to be of service to those who honor us by seeking our blessing upon one of the few really great experiences of their lives. The Reverend Roy A. Burkhart of Columbus, Ohio, insists that the couples he marries agree to come to him for a post-marital counseling session a few weeks after the wedding. Other ministers carry on their follow-up work in various other ways. The point is that if we are to make an impact on the marital situation in the future we must do more by way of preventing trouble than we have been doing.

B. *Marital Counseling*

More of our people suffer from marital difficulties than from any other single problem. This observation is misleading in that marital difficulties are never isolated but are an infinite number of interrelated problems; yet for purposes of analysis we oversimplify the actual condition. A large number of wives will say to you simply, "My husband and I are having trouble." This is the presenting symptom. It is up to the pastor to discover the underlying causes in order to help the parishioner understand the difficulty.

There are several ways in which the pastor may develop his marital counseling ministry. First he must prepare himself for this kind of work and be sure his attitude is one that will be helpful. If he is prejudiced toward the institution of marriage because of his own failure in marriage, or if he is concerned at the high divorce rate, then he will fail in his counseling in this field. The divorce rate is too low in light of the number of unhappily married people. There have been many studies made of the problem of marriage but, even so, most of the work remains to be done upon this subject, for we know so little about what makes a good marriage. What marital counseling is done is largely hit or miss, but even that is better than running away from the task as we often have done.

Due to the intimate nature of marital counseling and because of guilt feelings many of our people prefer to seek help from strangers. It is a matter of saving face. What man wants to admit he is ignorant of the emotional make-up of woman? Yet, woman herself is ignorant of her own make-up. Many a girl has fought shy of sex and of petting until she was married only to find that the reading of a wedding ceremony did not change her basic attitude toward sex and men; in marriage she was still afraid of them. The result is that sex to her is abhorrent. After a week or a month or a year, depending upon how smart she is, she recognizes that her husband's attitude toward her is changing but she does not know, or will not admit, why.

What woman likes to admit she has married a little boy who is still tied closely to his mother's apron strings? She does her best to break the tie but fails. Even in seeking counsel she often refuses to admit that she has failed; she tries to cover up her husband's immaturity out of loyalty to him and out of her own pride in herself.[2]

These conditions all combine to prevent wives from seeking pastoral help as well as sending them off to someone else for counsel. The pastor who reveals some understanding of the underlying problems that make for marital discord either in his preaching or in his talks to groups will have marital counseling to do.

The pastor who is not happily married himself will not work effectively in this field. Since the number of our pastors who are happily married would seem to vary little from the average, we may expect comparatively few ministers to be effective marital counselors. The same thing is more true of social workers, for most of them have never even been married.

Every pastor will, however, have some people who come to him for help because of marital unhappiness. He can carry through on the first phase of such counseling; he can listen passively. If the pastor feels uncomfortable while doing this work he should have enough interest in his parishioners to refer them to someone who can be of help.

In marital counseling the first task is to get the story of immediate unhappiness. This may be done with a few simple questions and some reassurance such as, "Feel free to talk frankly. You may be sure I will keep your confidence." When there are tears, as tears there usually are, a statement of reassurance such as, "Do not feel hurried, we have plenty of time," will help. Further questions as, "How long has this been going on?" "Have you ever been happy with your husband?" "How

[2] *Their Mothers' Sons*, Strecker, Lippincott, 1937.

long did you know each other before you were married?"
"How did you come to fall in love with each other?" "What
was the attitude of your family, of your husband's family,
toward the match?" "What kind of home did you have as a
child? Were your mother and father happily married?" "Were
your husband's mother and father happily married?" "How
do you know?" "Did you have other boy friends before your
husband?" "Did he have other girl friends?" "How did you
think about marriage as you were growing up?" "What did
you expect from marriage?" "Are your marital relations satisfying?" "What did you know about sex when you were married?" "If your marital relations are unsatisfactory, have you
ever consulted a physician?" Not all of these questions should
be asked, nor will they all be necessary, but some of them will
hit the trail of the difficulty. All are legitimate questions, however, whose answers should reveal the trouble.

A girl came to me saying she was going to get a divorce, that
she and her husband had never been happy, although they had
had two children together. I asked, "Why did you get married?" She replied, "I got married because my mother and father quarreled all the time." I asked, "What about your life
with your husband?" She said, "We have always quarreled."
She talked on for some time describing their differences of
opinion, many of which had to do with their attitudes toward
religion and social reform. The wife's description of her husband led me to believe he was a hard-working, conscientious,
complacent young man who was trying to get along in his small
community, while she wanted to change the world. I said,
"What about your marital relations?" She answered, "We have
none. He is impotent. He says I'm frigid. I don't want to have
anything to do with him. I want a divorce, but he has not
wanted to give it to me because of the children." I said, "What
do you want to do?" She said, "I want to be free to write. I'm
sure I can write." I said, "So you have made your husband frigid

so as to drive him to give you a divorce?" (This was a poor question because it was judgmental.)

A few months later she wrote, "Contrary to your advice I got a divorce. My ex-husband married his secretary two weeks later. I am very happy. The children are with me and I am spending my time writing." I had not told her she should not get a divorce; in fact I thought she should. I had pointed out some of the factors in the situation and she had not liked their looks. She had married to get away from home, but she made the mistake of having children before she went on to the next step in her search for freedom; or maybe it wasn't a mistake. Who can say!

A woman of fifty came for counseling concerning her marital situation. Her husband had repeatedly asked her for a divorce but would not take aggressive steps to secure one himself. The husband had failed in one position after another. The family lived frugally, but their three daughters had all been educated, one of them had married. The wife questioned whether she should agree to her husband's request for a divorce —she suspected that he had gone with other women at various times. My questions to her were, "How much does your marriage really mean? What will happen to your husband in case a divorce is secured? How much do you care?" She had come to a clergyman for counsel because she believed divorce wrong from a religious standpoint. Too often the church has been used to frustrate and suppress spiritual growth through insisting that mismated couples remain married even after it is recognized that they will not be able to reach a union emotionally through affection for each other.

We may expect an increase in marital counseling in view of the new independence which the war has brought for women. World War I opened many fields of industry for women; World War II opened an infinite number of others. This means economic independence so that the financial and moral double standard between men and women will increasingly disappear. Because of this new economic freedom women no longer need to take the abuse that men have heaped upon them. Before World War I, if she were not married a woman could become a domestic, a school teacher, or a nurse, and that was about all. Now she can enter any profession or field of industry. The result is that the divorce rate is mounting rapidly. In some cities one out of three marriages end in the divorce court. Some marriage counselors expect this figure to reach one out of two before it begins to decline. Here is a great need for intelligent pastoral counseling, for the emotional wear and tear upon the soul and body of marital disharmony is so great that it leads to mental and physical illness, to the destruction of morale, and to the warping of the lives of children who are born into homes which fail to give them the emotional support of a mother and father whose love for each other spills over into the lives of their children. The need for pastoral care in the field of marriage counseling is probably as great as in any other single area.[3]

C. Counseling with Young People

There is more interest in counseling with young people than with any other group, and there is more work being done by pastors in counseling with this group than with any other. The schools are carrying on an increasing amount of work in both vocational and therapeutic counseling but their programs are limited by the number of trained counselors who are available. For years the Young Men's and Young Women's Christian Association have carried on work of this nature with young people from a religious standpoint, which has been helpful in that their counselors have made up for lack of training through their genuine interest in the persons whom they attempted to

[3] *Christianity and the Family*, Groves, Macmillan, 1936.
When You Marry, Duval & Hill, Association Press, 1944.

help. In the large churches the pastors by necessity have usually delegated this important task to assistants.

A lad of seventeen told me of having gone to his pastor for help with a problem. He was in love, but his mother did not like his sweetheart; the mother insisted that the boy sit with the family at church while he wanted to sit with the girl. When he suggested to his mother that the girl sit with his family his mother had become angry and said she would not have them sitting together as if they "were engaged." The boy's father said little. Finally, the boy went to his pastor with his problem; the pastor listened to the story and then agreed to talk with the boy's father who was a member of his official board, but he did not carry out his promise. In describing his pastor to me the boy said, "He laughs at us and kids us about the things we go to him with. To us they are serious even though they may not seem so to him. Several of my friends have tried to talk to him but he treats them all the same way. None of us will go back to him."

Young people of high school age seek the pastor's help most frequently for vocational guidance. Even though they may be pretty well settled in the selection of their life work they are desirous of pastoral approval and encouragement. In some mysterious sense his approval, like his blessing in marriage, seems like the approval of God. As the pastor moves among his young people he ought constantly to be asking them, "What are your plans for the future?" This carries him into a discussion of life work, preparation and schooling, and frequently of boy-girl problems and marriage, because choosing a profession almost always involves delaying marriage past the time when the desire for marriage is strongest.

The Reverend Granger Westberg, chaplain of Augustant Lutheran Hospital in Chicago, while serving a local church, hit upon the plan of sending out cards to his Sunday School youngsters and young people inviting them to his study for conferences regularly every six months. He started with the seven-

year-old youngsters in Sunday school and worked up through
the young people in high school and then included his young
adults. The first time they came they were apprehensive, but
he soon put them at ease by explaining he wanted to get better
acquainted. The next time his card went out inviting them to
come, they came eagerly. His high-school-age students were
most responsive of all to this interest, especially as he talked to
them about their course of study and helped interpret it to
them. This also gave him an opportunity to discuss their life-
work plans. He got a one hundred per cent response in this
program from his Sunday School group and his young people
and approximately a ninety per cent response from students of
his denomination in the local college. Few of these students were
members of his church, but they welcomed his interest in them.

This program was launched with an announcement both
from the pulpit and in the church bulletin to the effect that
cards would soon go out to the Sunday School students and
young people inviting them to the pastor's study for an interview. The purpose of this program, he explained, was to enable
the pastor to get better acquainted with the youngsters individually. Announcements were also made through the Sunday
School and young people's society. Here is the card as Pastor
Westberg sent it out:

DEAR *GEORGE:*

Your pastor would like you to stop in at the church study for
a friendly visit on *Wednesday, April 6,* at *4:30 P. M.* If you happen
to be with a friend at the time feel free to bring him or her with
you. If you cannot come at the time indicated, kindly telephone
number *27* for a later appointment.

Sincerely,

GRANGER E. WESTBERG, *Pastor*

This card was mimeographed with italic portions written in.
The reasons for this was that this form gives the impression that
the call is impersonal in that everyone is getting a similar card;
also it is a time-saver.

This program has great possibilities as a method of launching a significant counseling program. It can work in almost any situation except in some rural churches. It has the advantage of being planned, orderly, and complete. Of course, no plan will work of itself unless it is worked. The counselor must have personality and skill enough to take advantage of the opportunity once the young people are in his study, all of which comes under the head of the art of counseling.[4]

When given the opportunity young people will want to discuss their choice of school and college. The pastor will need to know as much about special schools and courses of training as he can. For instance, many will never have heard about occupational therapy, or know that there are schools for the training of occupational therapists; neither will they have much idea about how to go about applying for acceptance to a school for specialized training. I am constantly amazed that top-notch young women, contemplating nursing, go to second- and third-rate nursing schools.

It is not that the average pastor will need to have information at his finger tips concerning vocations, schools and colleges, but he will know how to get information as it is needed while the young people and their parents will not. Many a youngster will receive little attention or encouragement from his parents as he attempts to make his plans. The pastor's interest in his future will be more important than the actual information which he gives. Selecting a life work and selecting a wife or husband are two of the three greatest decisions we make (the other being the decision to live a religiously creative life), naturally the pastor ought to be interested and helpful to his young people in these decisions.

When the pastor has established contact with his young

[4] Since this plan was published in the First Edition of *Pastoral Work and Personal Counseling* in 1945 many pastors and workers with young people have experimented with it. Chaplain Westberg and I would appreciate hearing from anyone who tries it regardless of whether the plan succeeds or fails. In this way we will be able to gather information and further improve the plan.

people and has shown his interest in them through inviting and keeping their confidences, they will come to him with their affairs of the heart, especially when those affairs become complicated. In the Reverend Mr. Westberg's plan the pastor knows of these affairs before they go bad and thus has the opportunity of being helpful before the individuals have become so seriously entangled that great suffering results. In counseling of this kind the pastor is helpful largely on the basis of what he can avoid doing. The church has been "against" so many things that young people have wanted to do and have done, not because pastors have been blind, but because the church is too often dominated by frustrated persons who have failed in practically everything they have done, including their own family life. The church leadership, therefore, cannot put into effect the kind of program they know young people need. Counseling which is done in a quiet, personal, inoffensive way can often offset the pastor's helplessness in other areas.

The mousy little girl who is not attractive and has every chance of becoming a wall flower—that girl who, as a woman, will find her way to the psychiatric clinic or into the homes of her more fortunate neighbors to be a slave for their children while her heart yearns for children of her own—is one who should be on the pastor's list. She will come for counseling only if he sends for her; for she will never dare to come otherwise. In facing such a girl the pastor will have difficulty in deciding what his responsibility is. Theoretically he should assume the problem is one of retardation and try to be of assistance until he has exhausted all possibilities. Many girls, if they are helped to understand how to use what the Lord has given them, can develop personal charm so as to overcome their lack of natural attractiveness. The psychologist believes that the person who persists in making herself unattractive does so with a purpose, oftentimes to punish a parent who has failed to give her a feeling of security through love. The pastor will be helpless in overcoming such an attitude in view of his limited amount of time and the tremendous demands upon it, but sometimes he will be able to enlist the aid of someone else in a girl's behalf so that she will come to know what real affection is even though she does not have it at home.

Young people, facing temptation and suffering from guilt feelings, will come to the pastor to talk about the situations in which they find themselves, particularly in their social relations, as new horizons open for them in high school, college, and business. There they see how others live, and come into close contact with young people whose standards are different from their own. A father showed me a letter from his son who was away from home serving in the army. He wrote, "I have not taken a drink although the boys often invite me to drink with them and a bartender offered to give me a drink. The girls are easy here. I wait outside the house until the others come out. I did not do those things at home and I will not do them here." Our hearts go out to that boy in the rugged loneliness of his determination to follow the ideals of his youth. He added, "You may pass this on to M. (his sweetheart), as I don't know how to write it to her."

Not all young people will have that boy's will power, many ultimately find their way to the pastor with feelings of guilt because they blame themselves for having been weak and think of themselves as unworthy of the affection of a lovely girl. It then becomes the minister's task to put them back on their feet so that they will be able to go on; their future need not be ruined by a lone episode, for life is not ruined except as we permit it to be.

The pastor is the one who will see these experiences for what they are, not tragedies that should wreck a life but suffering out of which spiritual strength may come, and will help re-establish a young man or young woman's self-respect through his ability to "see life steadily and see it whole." Through his perspective he will calmly listen to the story, taking plenty of time, letting the confession work itself through, being neither overly-eager with reassurance nor curious as to details of the experience.

Many young people will feel they must tell their beloved of their experience and break off their engagement. The pastor would be wise to suggest that such action not be hurried, but that adequate time be taken to think it through. While a few days will not alter the facts of the situation they may help a person to see the whole experience more calmly. I usually say, "I want to have a little time to go over this in my mind and then I want to see you again." If the youngster is quite emotional I make it the next day; if he seems relieved by our talk I make an appointment for two days later or even longer. In each instance I say, "If I were you I would not talk to anyone else just yet. We'll decide later about what you are to tell Mary." Actually there is no need to carry the story further to cause her suffering and raise doubts in her mind which she might not be able to handle.

Young people come to the pastor with problems of belief as they begin to broaden their understanding of the universe through the study of science and other subjects in school, and they seek reassurance from the pastor. Again, his help will turn upon his objectivity and the kind of understanding of counseling and of his universe which he has achieved. These problems afford him excellent teaching opportunities as well as counseling responsibility.

Counseling with young people, the youngsters of the early grades as well as high school and young adult age, calls for constant alertness on the part of the pastor to make opportunities for such contacts and to follow up the contacts as they present themselves. The pastor who cannot spend some time upon picnics, hikes, parties and banquets with his young people is missing a vital part of his pastoral responsibility; if they fail to seek his counsel he had better examine his ministry and re-budget his time.

D. *Counseling with Adults*

Adults will seek the pastor's help for various reasons, but regardless of the presenting story the basic problems will be those discussed in Chapter II. Therefore, I will point out only a few general observations here that have to do with counseling with adults.

Such counseling will grow out of routine calling, and from ideas that are gained from the pastor through his preaching concerning personal problems as discussed later in Chapter XI. Because of the growing popularity of counseling, it may be that the average layman soon will come to realize that the pastor can be of help to him as he faces personal crises. As our clergy become trained for this important task we will be able to carry on an educational program for the church at large to that effect. Setting up office hours is not enough, but office hours for the Protestant clergy will be necessary as counseling becomes popular, just as regular hours for confession are held by the Roman Catholic clergy. If the program of counseling with young people, initiated by Granger Westberg, comes into general practice, these youngsters, upon becoming adults, will come naturally to their pastor for personal counseling.

Here is a list of the problems with which adults have come to me most frequently. These overlap with those discussed elsewhere for the same type of problems may come to the pastor's attention whether he goes to the parishioner or whether the parishioner comes to him. In the latter instance our work is easier, for we have a different type of authority with the one seeking help and the parishioner recognizes he needs assistance even though he may be unwilling to follow through so as to actually achieve it.

1. Parishioners come to the pastor seeking employment. Sometimes work is actually what is desired and needed, and sometimes it is the excuse a parishioner will make for coming

to discuss something else. The pastor will do well to follow the rule of taking time and inquiring into the general spiritual condition of the parishioner. "How are things going?" "Why are you quitting your present job?" "Where have you worked?" "How is your family?" "What would you like most to do?" Any of these questions will open up the larger areas of a person's spiritual condition.

In dealing with need for employment the pastor should have business contacts and especially contacts with employment agencies to which he can send people. This should be a personal contact, not just a name in the telephone book, so that he can make whatever personal interpretation is necessary. The person who does not need some special help will find his own employment. In smaller communities such requests are not apt to come to the minister.

2. Another will be the person seeking relief. This request is becoming unusual in that public relief is well organized and information about relief agencies is so well known that our people make their own contacts directly. There will be occasions when supplementary relief is needed, which will come to the attention of the pastor either directly or through other parishioners. The pastor should have some funds available for such use; many churches make provision for such funds through special contributions made at communion services.

Special mention should be made concerning the person, usually a man, who comes to the pastor with a story, frequently on Sunday when the agencies are closed, and asks for two dollars or five dollars, to buy food, or a railroad ticket, or shoes, or something special. It is surprising how even the sophisticated pastors of large city churches fall for these "touches." A good rule is never to give out cash; all you need to do is to offer to buy the food that is asked for, or offer to call an agency where a "friend" of yours works, and your desperately needy person vanishes. If this seems a little cold-blooded to you take the trouble to spend time with a social worker and learn something about panhandlers and professional bums.

3. There are many who come seeking advice concerning a physician, simply because they do not know whom to call. Others will come because they are displeased with the medical care they are receiving and some will have a just complaint. The best procedure is to direct the parishioner to a good general practitioner rather than to a specialist; the specialist will be recommended by the general practitioner if one is needed. Exception to this is the obstetrician or the pediatrician, whom the pastor may recommend directly. Many communities will have only general practitioners, who do everything, including surgery. The doctor who never refers some surgery on to the great medical centers is one who may be looked upon as a poor diagnostician.

4. Parishioners will seek counsel concerning their mother or father, and sometimes both. This is apt to turn upon the question of what to do about mother now that father has died, as she has no place to go. Sister cannot take care of her and husband does not think she should live with us because of the children. This is a real problem and one that can make for difficulty. Elderly people are sensitive about being pushed off somewhere but plans usually can be made that are satisfactory to all. Sometimes the problem is simply that the daughter feels guilty because mother cannot live with her and needs reassurance from the pastor to the effect that mother should live elsewhere. In other generations when houses were large and when there was work for all, especially upon the farm, this was no problem, but in the city where people live in small houses and apartments and where there is less to do it is a difficult situation. The pastor needs to be fairly passive in his role but he can reassure a sensitive parishioner. On occasion he may even need to be positive in his support of the wishes of the son-in-law who feels that mother cannot live with them. At the same time he can seek

information concerning possible homes where elderly people can live comfortably. Old age pensions are causing many elderly persons to receive a welcome they did not have before.

5. Couples desiring to adopt a child should be referred to a good child-placing agency. Sometimes it is a matter of going to more than one. State adoption laws vary; there are still some where such agencies have low standards. Any agency, where there is a fee for the adoption of a baby and where little investigation is made of the prospective parents, is to be avoided. Again, it is a matter of securing information from a reliable social worker concerning child-placing agencies in a given community or recommending one elsewhere. Many agencies will give preference to a couple who come recommended by a pastor if the pastor is known and his judgment trusted. He should be certain that the couple seeking a child can give it love and emotional security. It is desirable for the pastor to make some inquiry as to why a couple desires to adopt a baby rather than have one of their own.

6. Parishioners often come to the pastor seeking help about a son or daughter who is having what they think is an unfortunate courtship which they fear will lead to a bad marriage. The parents are usually right but the situation is complicated by many factors. It is important to get the story as clearly as possible, being concerned particularly with the parents' attitude. In this problem we are of most assistance in trying to help parents keep the door open so that the youngster may return if she desires to when she realizes she has made a mistake; parents seldom want to lay down an ultimatum but feel they are forced to. You may say to parents, "Suppose they get married and their marriage fails; what will your attitude be?" Again, "Can you discuss the problem calmly with Mildred, or Jack?" Sometimes we are asked to try to break up an attachment and we should be willing to talk with the youngster and get his point of view, but to take sides in such a dispute is questionable even though we agree strongly with one or the other. The boy or girl who

asks our opinion seriously about a prospective wife or husband is in doubt. Our answer may be, "Why do you ask me?" thus giving the doubts an opportunity to come out into the open for examination. We should not make the decisions; but help to clarify the issues and bring some reason into a confused situation.

7. Parishioners will come to the pastor to discuss church problems and programs. Some few of them will concern the pastor's work directly in that they will have to do with a decision he has made, a program he desires, a sermon he has preached. This is apt not to be a counseling situation, but will have to do with the church school, the women's society, the official board, the church building or the budget. Sometimes the conference deals with the parishioner's difficulties—it may be a church school teacher who is having difficulty with a youngster and desires help, or a member of the women's society who was due to be elected president but was not. Perhaps it is a member of the choir who is not permitted to sing solos, or a member of the board who does not like a decision that was made. These and many other problems come to the pastor under the head of church program, but actually turn upon personality problems. The pastor's method is the same with practically all: listening, interpretation, reassurance, sometimes referral to someone else; all of which takes time and mental discipline.

8. Another problem that presents itself frequently is that of a wife who is concerned because her husband is drinking. If it is a case of heavy drinking, of true alcoholism, which is characterized by an uncontrolled drinking appetite where the individual drinks himself into unconsciousness with no ability to stop once he has started, the minister should suggest medical treatment. The results are not encouraging in such cases even with medical treatment. "Alcoholics Anonymous" is an organization comprised of former alcoholics who are having fairly good results with this problem; their organization is spreading steadily although as yet it is confined to the larger cities. In-

formation may be gained about their organization by writing to Post Office Box 658, New York, 8, New York.

If it is a case of social drinking that your parishioner describes, with some question in her mind about "other women," it is well to encourage her to tell you as much as she will about their marital life, including why they were attracted to each other and why they became married. Finally, it is well to inquire into the nature of their sexual adjustment; if this is unsatisfactory then referral to a physician for examination and sex counsel is in order. Mismarriage is one of the great causes of heavy drinking and the pastor cannot be helpful by attacking the problem of drink directly, neither does he need to counsel immediately with the husband, although this may be desirable eventually. If the husband refuses to cooperate and gives no intimation that he desires to change his behavior, then it is safe to assume that he is attempting to break up his marriage by his behavior and the wife should be helped to see that fact and accept it, for it takes two people to make a successful marriage.

9. The problem of homosexuality is another that will come to the pastor occasionally, so that he needs some understanding of it. Our society does not recognize that a third sex exists and we make no provision for such a fact in our thinking. Authorities, what few there are, differ upon the causes of homosexuality. They do agree, however, that the chances are slight of helping such a person to make a hetero-sexual adjustment. Such a person should be referred to a psychiatrist for counsel; if none is available in your community send him to a city where one is available. Do not waste time and run risks so far as your own reputation is concerned in dealing with something you know nothing about. There are no exceptions in dealing with this problem. It is not the pastor's problem; at the same time he can be sympathetic in urging a homosexual person to seek help elsewhere.

A number of these persons are attracted into the ministry and some few are ordained before their tendencies become strong;

some even marry and have children. Eventually their ministries are terminated, but not often without some unfortunate circumstances. As more adequate counseling facilities are made available in the theological seminaries these individuals will be spotted and directed out of the ministry into other types of work. Many are talented and have contributions to make to society. They cannot make them by becoming ministers, however, and none should be encouraged to try to work out their adjustments in this profession.

10. Marital counseling has already been discussed in a preceding section as a major problem that comes to the pastor.

11. Elderly people will find their way to the pastor's office, particularly if he encourages them to come. They come with various requests, sometimes with complaints or criticism, but their basic problem is apt to be loneliness and boredom, sometimes colored with paranoid feelings. In view of the tremendous, largely untouched problem of loneliness among elderly persons it is surprising how few do call the pastor or seek attention for themselves.

Counseling with adults is interesting because one hits problems with teeth in them more frequently than in counseling with young people, although there is deep soul-satisfaction in seeing youngsters develop and blossom out with help and encouragement. There is no such thing as a problem that is insignificant either among young people or adults; all are serious from the standpoint of the counselee, and it is from that standpoint that we must work.

PART FOUR

~~~~~~~~~~~~~~~~~~

PASTORAL WORK AND THE CHURCH

XI

PREACHING AND PASTORAL WORK

MOST CLERGYMEN THINK OF THEMSELVES AS CALLED "TO preach" and they give a major amount of their time and energy to the task of preaching. Preaching as the principal method of carrying on the work of the church is rapidly declining. Those communions that emphasized preaching and have been indifferent to other phases of the church's program are failing to hold their membership while other churches go steadily forward. The Church of the Latter Day Saints (Mormon) is one of the most rapidly growing religious groups in America. Every family belonging to the Mormon church is called upon every month by the elders (clergy) for the specific purpose of inquiring into the spiritual condition of that family. It is interesting that the Mormons were the only major religious group to take their members off the relief rolls during the depression of the twenties. The Southern Baptists, another rapidly growing denomination, have a strong religious educational program plus a constant emphasis upon personal evangelism, both of which contain the essence of fellowship as described in Chapter III. The Episcopal Church, where worship rather than preaching is emphasized, is a steadily growing communion and one that is holding its membership. In the Lutheran Church we find the happy combination of preaching, pastoral work, education and worship; it also is a steadily growing communion. One test of a communion is not whether it recruits new but whether it holds its old members.

Dr. Henry Sloane Coffin used to be fond of saying that it was not preaching but the "ringing of door bells" that built the great Madison Avenue Presbyterian Church in New York City which reached such heights of popularity during his pastorate there. But let no one be misled, Henry Sloane Coffin never neglected his preaching, and through the years he gave a major amount of attention to teaching the art of preaching to young ministers. While he has taught pastoral work he has never written upon the subject, much to the loss of American Protestantism.

It is not uncommon to find a minister who is described as a "weak" preacher but who is serving as pastor of an active and growing congregation. When examined carefully such a clergyman almost inevitably is found to have served that church for some years, during which time he has emphasized pastoral work. *His people love him.* The simple truths which he points out in his sermons are personal in their meaning to his listeners for he has been in their homes, stood beside their sick beds, rejoiced with them in good fortune and suffered with them in sorrow. He has baptized their babies, married their young people and buried their dead. But he has done more than conduct the formal services these functions require. He has known when a young mother was apprehensive, he has held homes steady when ship-wreck was threatened, he has brought affection to the aged and comforted the bereaved. His sermons hold truths for his people because he knows their needs and has known where to find the truths for those needs from the storehouse of religion. His preaching is effective because it helps people with the job of living, which is the acid test of preaching.

The preacher who draws his sermons from his own thought and from books but does not go about among his people, who never gives them an opportunity to tell him their thoughts, may have perfected the academic art of preaching, but he will fail as a preacher. It is like the physician who has mastered the subject of anatomy from the study of cadavers, but has never studied disease in living bodies.

A preacher always preaches about his own problems, it cannot be otherwise for such is the "growing edge" of his life. If he is a pastor his problems are his people's problems, therefore his sermons are realistic and, in so far as he knows the resources of religion, he is helpful in his preaching. The preacher's task is to bring into the lives of his people the Eternal Truth.

The clergyman who knows human problems but does not know Eternal Truth, God and the Ways of God, also fails in preaching. He is not a clergyman, he is a psychologist. The psychologist studies the human mind and human behavior; as a psychologist he makes no claim to a knowledge of God or of knowing how to bring God and man into harmony. In actual practice a clinical psychologist often serves as minister in that he does bring God and man together. God works through many, and oftentimes strange, channels.

One of the grave dangers of preaching is that the preacher may overshadow the truth he is talking about. Protestantism is characterized by the message; therefore the messenger is placed in the center of the church facing the people. Because of the frailty of the messenger he may glorify himself rather than God, so that people join the preacher rather than the church. When the preacher leaves that church for another, or for heaven, slight loyalty holds them in the church. If the pulpit is placed to one side of the chancel, if worship through communion, music, prayer and responses takes place, if God is glorified through the beauty of church architecture, if the religious heritage of the ages is present, then loyalty to God is apt to replace loyalty to a man. As pointed out elsewhere, pastoral work faces this same danger of glorifying the pastor.

Preaching is clergy-centered; pastoral work is parishioner-centered. It is difficult to bring the two together, but it is possible. Many who have concentrated upon preaching think of themselves as pastors, but they violate the basic practices of good pastoral work, as described in Chapter V, by talking about themselves, giving advice, reassurance, and manipulating their own ideas into the conversation or playing their personalities so that they dominate the parishioner. The role of the preacher is an individualistic one. While preaching, the clergyman is on his own; he makes or breaks that part of the service. It is true that the feeling of rapport between the preacher and the congregation inspires him to greater effort and strength. At the same time a part of the art of preaching is the ability to establish this feeling of friendliness between congregation and preacher. The clergyman who does not have that ability fails in his preaching. Rapport often rests back upon the pastoral work which has been carried on in the past. We like people who like us and who give us some attention. A physician said recently, "We have a new minister at our church. I've not been to hear him although he's been there three months. I had a birthday last week, and of all things here came a birthday card from the pastor. Guess I'll have to go round and hear him preach."

A major function of the pulpit is to carry on a teaching ministry. In this the relationship between pastoral work and preaching is strong and clear. One test of preaching is whether it brings people to the pastor to talk about their problems. The preacher who never has anyone come to see him or request him to call upon them or members of their family should examine his message and his pastoral work. This may necessitate consulting a counselor, particularly a psychiatric counselor, so that the preacher may gain some understanding of himself and why he is failing. Those preachers who are super-egotists and who are steaming along, attracting attention and having a wonderful time, will never consult a psychiatrist although many times their wives and children find it necessary. Such men not only help few people, but they definitely harm the cause of Christ and His Kingdom.

There are many sermons that will grow directly out of pastoral work, although the preacher must be careful of the kinds of illustrations he uses even though the experience took place in an entirely different congregation. The woman sitting in the second row who desires help in a marital situation that is going badly, the man sitting in the back pew who has been drinking because of his inability to turn in the number of orders his sales manager expects, the high school boy sitting in the balcony, will think, "He talks about other people, he makes wise cracks about their troubles, he would talk the same about me," and they go away sorrowing. The minister can deal with personal problems without citing illustrations such as, "I met a woman and she said to me——."

A sermon titled, "The Resources of Religion in Time of Trouble," may deal with faith and the strengths of faith, why doubt comes and how faith is gained and actually strengthened through trouble. Go to the history of Israel for illustrations, go to Jeremiah and Hosea, to the Gospels, to Paul, to John Bunyan, to John Baxter; biographical literature is filled with illustrations of the triumph of faith in the midst of suffering.

A sermon upon, "The Returning Son and the Forgiving Father," would develop around the parable of the Prodigal Son, and would be directed toward those suffering from a sense of guilt and failure. Here we see the Mind and Nature of God more clearly than at any other place in the New Testament. Most people are not sinners in the sense that they consistently and persistently work at the job; those people are seldom in the church, although their wives may be. The average person indulges in minor sins and may not feel his religion is helpful because he is so uncomfortable when he comes to church.

"The Ability to Accept God" would be a sermon that would afford the pastor an opportunity to point out the defensive nature of persons who have known emotional insecurity at home. How can a person love God or permit God to love him who has heard his mother and father quarrel all his life, who has been bullied by his older brother and father and who has never had anyone put his arms around him and say, "I love you, Little Man."

Ministry to the sick starts in the pulpit. Our people should be instructed about what to expect from the pastor in time of illness and death. In such a sermon the minister may say simply, "When I call upon you when you are ill we will talk about what you want to talk about. We will tell stories if you desire, but you will have to tell the first one. If you want to tell me how you feel about your suffering, your discouragement, your embarrassments, your failures you will have the opportunity to do so. And of this you may be sure: I will listen and be interested in whatever you tell me. And further, whatever you tell me will not be told to another. We know that talking with someone in whom you have confidence about what is worrying you or what has happened to you, helps you to become free of it emotionally, to get it out of your mind, to conquer it. There is no event so insignificant, no fear so small but that it is important to me, if it is to you. When I call upon you when you are sick we will have prayer if you want to. The prayer is for you. It is not that your pastor's prayer is to replace yours, or that mine will have more influence with God. Rather it is that I stand free from your suffering. I am able to see life steadily and see it whole which, as a sick person, whose perspective and vision are limited, you cannot. I am able to be calm and relaxed which in itself helps you to permit God to bless you with confidence and calmness, therein aiding you in the recovery of health.

"The same thing is true if you are sick unto death. It is to be hoped that you will have made your peace with God long before you come to die. But dying is a lonely experience, your body is fighting disease, your mind is confused by drugs. Foreign thoughts lay hold upon your mind as bacteria lay hold upon your body. My prayer serves to reassure you, to drive out doubts as medicine drives out disease, to remind you and make real to you again the things you believe but have forgotten.

"Finally, remember: I am as near to you as the telephone, at any hour of the day or night. If you call me I will rejoice in the opportunity you have given me, in the trust you have placed in me, through your asking me to call. We may not solve your problem, but in so far as you are able to seek and accept help, we will strengthen you in your efforts to live with your problem. Try as I will I am not able to know you are sick unless you send me word. You will notify the ice man, the milk man, and the paper boy, perhaps you will remember also to notify your pastor when you are ill, and going to the hospital." I venture to suggest that such a sermon will be remembered a long time, especially if it is repeated, in one way or another, about once each year.

The subject of suffering should be much in our sermons; the Christian conception needs constant interpretation. Vague and negative preaching about evil and sin is largely a waste of time. Our people do not need to be told we are against evil: that they may assume. And to run in our pet idea as a filler because we have nothing else to say is a sure sign of too many committee meetings and too little pastoral work during the past week.

XII

THE MINISTER AND PSYCHIATRY

PSYCHIATRY IS ONE OF THE NEWEST SPECIALTIES IN THE MEDI-cal profession. While as a specialty it dates back a hundred years, still its great advance was made between the two world wars, until now its pronouncements upon human behavior and its observations upon human personality are listened to by leaders in every field of industry and in every profession.

Psychiatry as a term comes from the Greek and means *mental healing;* psyche means soul, hence, *soul healing.* For thousands of years both the treatment of the body and the soul were in the hands of the clergy. Gradually, with the development of medicine, first the treatment of the body and then the treatment of the mind were turned over to the doctor; because the bodies of those who were seriously deranged mentally had to be cared for by the physician, he gradually came to take over the care of the mind also.

Originally the doctor was interested largely in the sickness or symptoms which the patient presented, not in the patient himself. Emil Kraepelin, often called the father of psychiatry, classified the symptoms into categories that are still used in general. As mental symptoms began to make sense to the observer and as treatment slowly emerged, psychiatry became more interested in the person with the disease until he finally came to claim, as he now does, that his field of study and treatment is *the total person.* For centuries mental illness, like physical illness, was interpreted as punishment for wrong-doing and the individual whose behavior was "peculiar" or "different" was thought to

148

be demon-possessed. This interpretation of behavior held until almost the contemporary period, and even today great numbers of our laity believe that both physical and mental suffering is sent upon them as punishment. In 1810, a hundred and forty years ago, a group of Boston physicians decided to enlist public support for the establishing of a hospital, as there was none in New England at that time. A letter was composed and sent to selected Boston citizens, signed by a clergyman, in which this revealing sentence appears, "We desire to found a hospital for the care of idiots and other patients." As a result the Massachusetts General Hospital was founded, of which the McLean Hospital, now in Waverly, Massachusetts, is for the care of the mentally ill. Much progress has been made since 1810 in the understanding and treating of those who were called "idiots" at that time.

Psychiatry now claims to treat *the total person;* actually this is a ridiculous claim because no one physician can know enough to treat the total person. In our book, *The Art of Ministering to the Sick,* Richard Cabot, M.D., wrote, "If you see a sign above a doctor's office which reads 'physician-surgeon', look for another doctor, for no one can be smart enough to be both physician and surgeon." In actual practice the psychiatrist treats the soul and depends upon other medical specialists to diagnose and treat the major physical ills of his patients.

The clergyman watched the growing influence of the psychiatrist with mixed feelings as he saw more and more of his people turn to psychiatry for help upon the very problems which he had sought to interpret through the centuries. He did not become alarmed, however, so long as the psychiatrist dealt primarily with the seriously deranged, for while his forefathers in the faith had believed a psychotic person to be demon-possessed, modern man did not believe demonology an adequate explanation for either mental or physical illness. So it must have been with a sense of relief that the late medieval clergyman gave over the care of the mentally ill to the doctor. But when, following the work of Sigmund Freud, a Jewish psychiatrist, who rejected both his parental religion and his father's domination as being one and the same, and who through his brilliant observations moved to the study of interpretation of spiritual problems, striking out as he did so at Judaism, Christianity and other religions,[1] both authoritarian and autocratic, the clergyman became alarmed.

Psychoanalysis has been the great observer and interpreter of personality and human behavior of our generation; ninety per cent of all psychiatric thinking and practice is psychoanalytic, even though there are only approximately 400 recognized psychoanalysts in America, while there are 4000 psychiatrists. Many clinical psychiatrists claim they reject psychoanalysis, yet they constantly use its insights and its discoveries.

Many varied claims are made about psychoanalysis even by its friends, while the attacks by its enemies are so impassioned and bigoted that they are not worth serious consideration. Some of its friends and followers claim it is a technique for research and treatment and nothing more, that it is not a philosophy and that one can be orthodox or liberal theologically, Jew or Christian, Catholic or Protestant. Actually followers of all these types of thinking and of no formal theology are practicing psychoanalysts. For others it is a complete philosophy, and they make little effort to interpret the meaning of life and the universe beyond that made by psychoanalysis.

The followers of Freud have been prolific teachers, writers, propagandists, for they have believed their findings were vitally important for their generation, so they have gone forth, particularly through books, into the highways and by-ways, spreading the "good news." Some have been true to the "historic faith" and have sought faithfully to reproduce it; while others, like evangelists of other faiths, have paused to brood, to observe in their own right, and to make additions to the writings of the

[1] *The Future of an Illusion*, Freud, Liveright, 1928.

founder; some have even been so bold as to suggest that they make corrections.

During this same period of historic conquest for the gospel of psychoanalysis, the Christian church, in its various branches, has been particularly sterile; its energy was consumed in hurrying in one direction and then another, through struggling to to apply a horse-and-buggy theology to an airplane age. Slowly its influence slipped away. The care of souls, which is its business, suffered, for it had lost its old authority and had failed to develop a new. Naturally the clergy were suspicious and defensive toward psychoanalysis and psychiatry as they moved forward to—by their own claim—"treat the total person," particularly when the psychiatrist considered the clergyman an enemy rather than an ally. A movement or a nation is apt to feel that way when it invades the territory of another.

The clergyman said that psychiatry denied God. It did no such thing. The psychiatrist said that the clergyman denied science and the scientific method. He did no such thing. The clergyman said that the psychiatrist encouraged people to stay away from church and to deny the historic faith. He did no such thing, except in some instances where the church, in the person of the pastor, and the domination of the patient's parent or parents, was causing illness and blocking the forces of health. The psychiatrist claimed that the pastor was autocratic, dogmatic and authoritarian; some were, but not all, by any means. The clergyman claimed the psychiatrists encouraged their patients toward sexual promiscuity; a few may have but more often the patient broke both with his church and his psychiatrist when he indulged in such practices. The psychiatrist said religion caused guilt feelings which resulted in mental illness because of its emphasis upon sin. It is the task of religion to describe life as it may be lived and to hold up goals of purposefulness in living. Guilt feelings do result when individuals fall short of those goals. The capacity to feel guilty and to have a sense of failure is one of the things that distinguishes man from other creatures of the field. The psychiatrist often seems not to have recognized this fact. Naturally religion leads to some guilt feelings; it is too strong a feeling not to. It may also lead to health.

So we see both psychiatry and the ministry at fault in misunderstanding and misinterpreting each other, while the real cause of the difficulty was that each threatened the other. At the same time the real concern of each was the care of persons or helping people. It is around this concern and across this bridge that psychiatry and the ministry meet: the youngest and oldest disciplines in the care of the souls. Fortunately there are courageous practitioners in both disciplines who are more concerned about the truth than they are about the weaknesses of the opposing tradition, about suffering people than they are about their own financial and professional gain. While there is more that we do not know than we do about the mutual strengths and weaknesses of psychiatry and the ministry, the similarities and dissimilarities, we know enough to lead us to believe that the two should be allies and not enemies, that they should work together rather than struggle against each other.

This is written for the clergyman, therefore I shall describe how the psychiatrist can be of help to the minister rather than vice versa; as a matter of fact I know far more about this part of the subject than I do of the other for I have sent more people to the psychiatrist than I have had sent to me by the psychiatrist. While some would say this is regrettable the truth of the matter is that the psychiatrist has been far more helpful in pointing out how he works and how he gains his results than has the clergyman, and until the psychiatrist understands our role better than he does at present we will not see the balancing of the referral ledger.

In this connection we must recognize that one of the difficulties of cooperation between the two professions, and one of the reasons that it is easier for the pastor to refer people to the psychiatrist than it is the other way around, is that the psychiatrist works upon a fee basis while the pastor does not. This is no easy problem and at present I do not see a solution to it. I have never charged a fee for counseling whether a person was sent by a psychiatrist or not; some of my clergy friends have. As a practical problem, so far as concerns the average clergyman, who looks to the psychiatrist as one who can help him with his problems, this is not serious, for the psychiatrist does the work and charges the fee. The pastor does the referral and both he and his parishioner expect that a fee shall be charged.

The minister needs to be interested in psychiatric symptoms and diagnosis so that he will know whom to refer to the psychiatrist, and so that he will avoid making serious mistakes in his ministry to people who need more specialized care than he can give. He is the only professional person who moves freely among a large number of people and is in position to spot emotional troubles in their incipient stages, particularly in youngsters. Many a child who is thought of as a model youngster is moving steadily toward serious emotional trouble, while many an adult who is thought of as eccentric is actually suffering from a deep-seated mental illness; even more serious is the person who seeks the pastor's help just before committing suicide. The minister must know that physiological changes affect the personality, and that the alcoholic has no more control over his actions than the patient suffering with pneumonia has conscious control over the disease within his body.

Psychiatric problems fall into the following general classifications: the psychotic, the neurotic—coming to be called the psychoneurotic, and emotional problems associated with organic conditions. The psychotic is one suffering from such serious emotional difficulty that he loses contact with reality, cannot do his work and often must be hospitalized. The psychoneurotic is one whose emotional illness, which is due to an unsolved unconscious conflict, may interfere with his work and his life in general but he knows who he is, where he is, and when it is; that is, he is oriented in person, place, and time, as the psychiatrist would say, but he may still misinterpret reality. In between the psychotic and psychoneurotic is the great, gray borderline in which the symptoms are not clear enough to make a definite diagnosis possible: these are the problems that fool the minister, and often the psychiatrist. The important thing for the clergyman to remember, however, is that a definite diagnosis is not as important as recognizing that he is dealing with an emotionally *sick* person.

A number of different organic conditions bring about a change in personality and behavior; some of these changes are mild, others severe, some masquerade in one cloak of symptoms and some another. Essential hypertension, arteriosclerosis (hardening of the arteries), tumors of the brain, injuries to the head, encephalitis, general paresis (caused by syphilis), alcoholism, and other physical conditions cause mental and emotional changes. While the immediate cause of an alcoholic's behavior is organic, the roots of his trouble are emotional or functional. This problem, along with that of the person given to drug addiction, would fall into the gray borderland between the psychoneuroses and the organic; basically it would be classified as an emotional problem.

The major psychotic problems which concern the minister most are the *manic-depressive psychoses*, the *dementia praecox* or *schizophrenias* and the *paranoias*. In the true manic-depressive psychosis there are two phases: the excited and the depressed, although the depressed condition is the one the minister is most apt to see, for often the depressed person realizes something is wrong and seeks the minister's help. The person suffering from a *simple depression* presents a picture of sadness, is melancholy and worries over past minor misdemeanors, depreciating himself as being worthless. Tears often accompany his story and he claims that life is not worth living. The *acutely depressed* person may become stuporous, refusing to eat, claiming that he has committed the unpardonable sin.

Both these persons are seriously ill emotionally and must be gotten to a psychiatrist at once. If no psychiatrist is available they should be *taken* to a general physician for further advice and consultation. The seriousness of the situation must be impressed upon the family for these persons *commit suicide,* regardless of whether they talk about it or not. It is a mistake to believe, as many do, that the person who talks about suicide does not do it. Regardless of whether a person talks about suicide or doesn't, if he is depressed get him to a psychiatrist. Let someone else decide how sick he is.

The manic phase of this psychosis is characterized by excitement and exaggeration. A reasonable and reliable person begins to work fourteen and sixteen hours a day, becomes loud and talkative, negotiates business deals which he is incapable of carrying through and enters into propositions that are far beyond his financial capacity. That person is as sick as if he had pneumonia.

The hopeful thing about persons who become either excited or depressed is that many of them get well in time with or without treatment. With shock treatment the length of time of their suffering can be greatly shortened.

The second major psychotic group that the minister must be alert for are those suffering from dementia praecox or schizophrenia. This is an emotional problem of young people coming on in the late teens and twenties. It forms the bulk of hospital cases, from 15 to 20 per cent of new admissions being with this diagnosis; further, these cases stay in the hospital a long time.

Dementia praecox means *premature dementia* or early deterioration of mental powers. The term schizophrenia, now used more widely, means "splitting" of the personality. The patient's mind is fragmented, or divided, he loses his identity as a person—often speaking of himself in the third person, "He said he would do it," "He recognizes you as a friend." The onset of this disturbance often presents itself through a preoccupation with religious ideas, "the voice of God," or "the will of

God," which directs the patient to do certain things. The sufferer will not seek the pastor's help himself, for he often withdraws from social contacts, having little understanding of what is happening, but the family or friends frequently bring the pastor into contact with the patient. When this happens the minister should advise the family to seek the help of a psychiatrist, as this person is seriously ill and is irresponsible for his acts.

There are several forms of dementia praecox. The *hebephrenic* is the most common, and is characterized by rapid, nonsensical talking, with delusions, and often excitement. The *catatonic* type is apt to come on rapidly, is characterized by periods of stupor, loss of interest in usual activities, and peculiar mannerisms; the patient may stand or sit in one position for a long time, even though it is uncomfortable, and may refuse to control or perform bodily functions. The *paranoia* may come on later than the other types, and is characterized by feelings of persecution, ideas of grandeur and delusions of various kinds, usually of a fantastic and illogical nature. The *simple dementia praecox* patient is not often hospitalized, and is one who has mild symptoms, is slightly paranoid, does not have delusions and gets along fairly well.

The *paranoiacs* cause the minister no end of trouble for they are not people that he can help nor can get out of his hair. These people are seldom hospitalized for very long and in some instances they are definitely dangerous. However, they are more of a threat to one's reputation than to one's life. This emotional trouble is characterized by a belief that the subject is being discriminated against and persecuted. They are often educated and intelligent persons. The psychoanalysts believe paranoia is due to some deficiency in the sexual sphere, as sexual delusions are found in many persons suffering from paranoia. Since everyone is slightly paranoid the minister should expect to meet this problem often.

The psychoneurotics interest the minister more than those who are more seriously ill, but they are almost as hard to help as the psychotics. The pastor needs to have their symptoms in mind. The *obsessive compulsive neurotic* is one who follows a pattern of behavior which he does not understand and cannot control, such as excessive handwashing, picking up pins on the sidewalk, stepping over cracks in the sidewalk, always putting his right shoe on first. The compulsions may be harmless or they may become quite incapacitating. This neurosis has been called the borderland between neurosis and psychosis. Cases of compulsive neurosis should always be referred to a psychiatrist as this neurosis often is a defense against a schizophrenic breakdown. The *anxiety neurosis* is characterized by excessive and persistent worry, tears and inability to apply oneself to one's work. There is the recognition of the unreasonableness of the fear by the patient but still the subject has no control over the feeling. This is the most common of all the psychoneurotic manifestations. *Neurasthenia* is a condition characterized by symptoms of "nervous exhaustion" or "fatigue"; this is a type of behavior often seen in persons who are not equal to the job of living. *Hysteria* is associated with excitement. Its chief characteristic is the changing of an idea, which for some reason is unacceptable, into a physical symptom. Thus the diagnosis is most often made by doctors who are unable, after careful examination, to establish a physical cause for a complaint. The *psychopathic personality* is sometimes called "the waste-basket" diagnosis by psychiatrists. This is the person who, while completely oriented, is just asocial. These persons are usually well-groomed, pleasant, agreeable, charming individuals who have no social sense or moral responsibility. They will lie to you, steal from you, and knife you in the back with pleasure. The minister will have difficulty identifying the psychopath and will usually be "taken in" by him.

The homosexual may or may not be emotionally sick. The minister will often come across him for he expects the clergyman to be more tolerant of him than are others. He is one who, for reasons that are beyond his control, regardless of their original onset, prefers members of his own sex for his sexual experience. These persons may or may not be disturbed by such feelings and they are often useful and creative persons. The pastor will do well not to break his heart in trying to change their desires. Such people should be advised to go to big cities rather than staying in small communities, where they inevitably get into trouble.

This is a sketchy description of some of the emotional problems the minister faces and with which the psychiatrist can help. Increasingly the minister and psychiatrist must join hands in interpreting and serving the emotional needs of our people. Emotional problems have their roots in man's experience in trying to reach a reconciliation with his environment, and in his efforts to live creatively in a world which he believes may be friendly but often finds hostile. This also is the area of human experience in which the pastor works. One of his greatest contributions is in demonstrating through his person and the church, as a fellowship, that the universe *is* both *friendly* and *creative*.[2]

[2] *Handbook of Psychiatry*, Overholser and Richmond, Lippincott, 1947.
Understandable Psychiatry, Hinsie, Macmillan, 1948.
You and Psychiatry, Menninger and Leaf, Scribners, 1948.
The Human Mind, Menninger, Third Edition, Knopf, 1946.
Psychiatry for Everyman, Brown, Philosophical Library, 1947.
Emotional Problems of Living, English and Pearson, Norton, 1945.
Psychoanalysis for Teachers and Parents, Anna Freud, Emerson Books, 1947.
Mind and Body, Dunbar, Norton, 1947.
The Rights of Infants, Ribble, Columbia, 1943.
Mental Illness, A Guide for the Family, Stern, Commonwealth Fund, 1945.

XIII

THE CLERGYMAN AND OTHER
PROFESSIONAL WORKERS

THE PHYSICIAN, THE NURSE, SOCIAL WORKER AND CLERGYMAN are the four major humanitarian professional workers. Two of these professions are dominated by men and two by women. Because of their emotional make-up women have a difficult time in medicine just as they do in the ministry. There are few men case-workers, although many men are serving as administrators in social work. There are few men nurses. Women who go into medicine and the ministry usually are masculine in temperament, while men who become social workers and nurses are effeminate in temperament. As a matter of fact men who are physicians and clergyman are more sensitive by nature than are men of other professions; it is this sensitivity that gives them an awareness of human suffering and makes the alleviation of suffering vital to them.

In addition to these four professional groups there are others who give some attention to work with spiritual problems through counseling. The attorney does some work in this field, although the extent and quality of his work is difficult to measure. The consulting psychologist, the college counselor and the occupational therapist are still numerically small and their training and effectiveness vary greatly. Because the group is small not much need be said about them except to point out that such professions do exist and that their members are at work in the field of counseling.

We may expect both college counseling and occupational therapy programs to increase in the future. The newest development in the humanitarian field is the appearance of the personnel worker in industry. He is a combination of clergyman, psychologist and ward-heeler. His task is not yet clearly defined and his training is not established. In some situations he hires and fires, in others he does not; often he is the bridge between employer and employee; he works with human problems as they affect the worker and production; therefore, he may be said to be working partially in the field of pastoral care. His coming marks a new day in industry and we may expect to see personnel departments eventually accepted throughout industry, whether it be in factories where goods are manufactured or in hospitals where bodies and souls are healed. The personnel worker has the opportunity of the pastor to minister to individuals without the burden of a budget or a ladies aid society.

Among physicians there exists a plan of consultation, wherein two or more doctors examine a patient and then, through discussion together, decide upon diagnosis and treatment. Likewise the clergyman may hold such consultation in behalf of a parishioner. This may be with a physician, a public health nurse, a personnel worker in industry, an attorney, or a social worker. As life in our modern society becomes increasingly complicated, the pastor cannot expect, nor need he feel obliged, to carry full responsibility for a parishioner whose life becomes tangled to the point of needing help. It must be remembered, however, that the individual decides whom he will select as his spiritual adviser. As professional people we may make elaborate plans, we may have highly skilled training, we may agree who shall do what and how, but the individual will make the final choice as to how he shall be helped, if and when he desires help.

The clergyman needs to recognize that there are others who work in the spiritual area besides himself. He need not become apprehensive lest he lose his flock. If he is dealing with life realistically and helpfully, he will have work to do.

We often see an attitude of possessiveness among professional people toward their patients, clients, parishioners. It is *my* patient, *my* client, *my* parishioner, and resentment is expressed toward anyone else entering into the emotional picture. This is a sign of emotional immaturity and insecurity on the part of the worker. Far better is the attitude I heard expressed recently by a pastor who said, "I do not care where they get it so long as they receive what they need."

A. *The Clergyman and Physician*

Formerly the doctor and minister were contained in the same person, in the tribal medicine man; as such, he gave more attention to the care of the soul than he did to the body. Trouble in the body meant that there was trouble in the soul.

As the healing art began to be practised separately from organized religion it is not surprising that the church fought its development. The old always struggles against the new, for the new is a threat to the existence of the old. An interesting example of the struggle between religion and medicine took place in England; when anæsthesia first began to be used to relieve the pain of childbirth the English clergy protested, claiming that such a practice was against the laws of God. Woman had sinned in the Garden of Eden and God had cursed her through the pain of childbearing; if it had been meant to be otherwise, they said, childbirth would have been free from pain. This controversy continued until an English physician pointed out that in the Genesis story of creation God Himself had used anæsthesia in that He had caused Adam to fall into a "deep sleep" when Eve was created from the rib of Adam. After that the controversy quieted down.

More progress has been made in the last hundred years in the relief of physical pain than in all the rest of human history.

Scientific medicine is less than a hundred years old. The doctor welcomed its advent with enthusiasm. "Now," he said, "I can treat disease. Now I can be free from that troublesome creature, the patient. All I want from him is that he pay his bill." So the doctor of the twentieth century went about the practice of scientific medicine, only to find that if disease were treated without treating the patient, his bill was not paid and all too often the patient did not get well. Today the physician is recognizing that both disease and patient must be treated if good results are to be obtained.

The doctor holds as his task, "the alleviation of suffering and the prolongation of life." What the individual does with life when he has it the physician is not inclined to ask. He would be content, and often is, with the treating of symptoms, or the relief of physical pains. The conscientious physician, who conceives of his task in the broadest sense, who is motivated by a genuine affection for his fellow creatures, is not content with treating symptoms. He desires to see life lived happily and creatively because, in helping to achieve that condition, the joy of sound work comes to him; as a scientific man he has observed that disease is defeated where there is purposefulness in living. He gains little satisfaction in bringing about a cure of disease in a prostitute, knowing that upon the recovery of her health she will return to her sordid trade; yet as a physician his work includes the sinner as it does the saint. As a practical human being, but not as a physician, he does ask, "What are you going to do with health when you have it?"

That is the question the clergyman asks also, only he speaks of *life* instead of *health*. Theoretically the clergyman is interested primarily in quality of living while the physician is interested in quantity of living. The clergyman, because he believes in a love of God that is not limited by time, does not care greatly when you die, except as your death affects your loved ones, for he believes that in death your life and work

OTHER PROFESSIONAL WORKERS

continue and he does not think of that as tragic. The physician's task is to keep you living as long and with as little suffering as possible; the clergyman's task is to help you live creatively and turn even your suffering and death into triumphant experiences.

In actual practice the physician and clergyman often are working upon the same specific problems. Because of the gap between the two professions which was increased with the coming of scientific medicine, and because of the lag in the training of clergymen for the practical task of ministering to individual persons, the doctor and minister have worked independently of each other to the patient-parishioner's detriment. The instance of a doctor and minister came to my attention who were both trying to prevent a man from committing suicide. Each thought that he was the only one who knew of the man's trouble. United in the task through consultation together they presented a strong combination.

A significant factor which makes it difficult in some instances for the physician and clergyman to work together is that the two make their livings in different ways. The doctor is paid by the individual patient, the minister is paid by a group; even so, I have never found it difficult to work with a successful doctor, nor with one who was really interested in his patient's welfare. These are men who feel economically and emotionally secure with their patients while the doctor who feels possessive is one who has but few patients. Exceptions to this rule are the doctors who have had a bad time with a clergyman in other cases, or who have a sense of guilt toward the church because of their own past experience with it. Many physicians, who never go near churches, are deeply religious men. They have a profound respect for nature and the dependability of nature. The sincere physician is a religious man, even though he may not openly profess his faith.

Marked gains have been made in bridging the gap between

the physician and clergyman; as we define our tasks more clearly and have a better understanding of each other's methods this gap will close more completely.

As clergymen we need to recognize that the physician is employed to assist a person to recover his health and is responsible for the patient during that time. He may be discharged by the patient or the family but he is responsible so long as he is employed. Therefore, if the clergyman comes into the picture he does so only with the physician's consent. The relationship between our two professions has been such that as ministers we seldom are barred from the sickroom, and we rarely bother to obtain the physician's specific consent to call upon his patient. Likewise, seldom does the physician request our assistance. Until we reach the time when our mutual tasks are more clearly understood we would do well to be certain that we do as little harm as possible in the sickroom, and we must remember that the physician is employed to run the case and is responsible for doing so.

A telephone call to him, telling him you are Mrs. Blank's pastor and that you wonder how you can be most helpful to her, will reassure the physician concerning your judgment. If there is some question in your mind about your ministry he will often have ideas as to how you can help. You may have known her for years while he will have known her only a few days; even so, he may know her better than you do. Likewise, the clergyman needs to be cautious about advising a parishioner to go to a church hospital unless the local physician consents. A clergyman may become very unpopular in his community with the physicians because he advises everyone to go to the hospital of his communion.

Ideally, the physician, *not the clergyman,* as Dr. Richard Cabot said in our book, *The Art of Ministering to the Sick,* is the general. The doctor will decide what is needed for a patient even though he will not suggest specifically how the clergyman shall proceed with his task. That is, the doctor will think of the minister as working to strengthen a patient's morale, which may effect a recovery; he will not decide whether the clergyman's method should be listening, prayer, or communion. Just as he turns to the surgeon for a particular type of work, so he will turn to the clergyman.

In Chicago a woman was brought into the hospital by her minister because her local physician had told the minister he was unable to help her further. The local pastor asked me to see her so that I knew her from the time of her admission. She gave a history of prolonged abdominal pain, also a past history of five or six operations, the reasons for which appeared questionable to our physicians. They were questionable in that they were the kind a persistent patient could trick a surgeon into performing. Even though our physicians doubted that the woman had organic disease they decided to do a complete physical examination. To their surprise the X-ray examination revealed a small tumor of the lower bowel. They felt it improbable that this tumor should have caused her abdominal distress but decided to operate. Surgery of this nature often is a psychologically mutilating procedure in that the diseased segment of bowel is removed and an artificial anus is made through the wall of the abdomen so that defecation takes place through the patient's side. From the standpoint of psychic shock this is one of the most serious surgical procedures done, and yet hundreds of them are performed every year and the patients respond quite satisfactorily.

The operation was performed upon our patient and the surgeon was pleased at what he was able to accomplish. The tumor proved to be cancer, but it was in its early stages. Convalescence is slow in these cases, but in this one it was particularly slow; the patient just would not fight. Finally, she was sent home, only to return later with many complaints, among which was one concerning her heart.

I had been seeing her regularly, and had had prayer several times with her. She was responsive, but I always left with a feeling of discouragement. After her return to the hospital the internist (general physician), the surgeon and I got together for a consultation. We decided upon drastic psychic treatment. She was to be told by the surgeon that she had had a cancer (she had always been afraid of cancer), that the cancer had been removed, that she could live six months or ten years, but that if she continued as she was she would not only kill herself but her husband also. My role was to swing her mind away from herself and build up her morale in any way that I could. We were unable to decide how well we succeeded, but we feel we did not get far. We were hampered because our treatment was too superficial. What she needs is a complete psychoanalysis to enable her to understand herself and her attitudes and that is not available.

The physician and clergyman strengthen each other's work to the benefit of the patient when they work together; when they work independently of each other the patient is not best served. A physician friend of mine, Dr. Paul Ledbetter of Houston, Texas, has said repeatedly, "The cat is on the back of the clergy. When they are prepared to handle emotional problems of the patient the doctor will gladly welcome them as co-workers." He is absolutely right. When the clergy comes to understand its task in the sickroom, as in the whole field of pastoral care, the physician will welcome him as a co-worker.

B. *The Clergyman and Nurse*

It is not unusual for the nurse to know the patient better than the physician does. She is in and out of the patient's room many times a day, while the physician comes only for a few minutes. When the doctor enters the room the patient often responds to his interest and may appear better than he is; when the nurse comes in the patient relaxes into his true mood.

Some of the pastor's most important requests to see patients come from nurses. The nurse is a friendly person; she has to be or she fails as a nurse. Since she is trained to work with her hands, her mind works in a direct way. If she has seen the clergyman help one person she believes he might help another, so she calls him. It is that simple. If she sees a patient weeping she inquires why the tears and sets out to do something about them. Since she is a person of action she is apt to be aggressive in the spiritual area. If you encourage her to call you when your parishioner is discouraged she will do so and not know or care how busy you are. It is your job to help people and she will expect you to do it. If you inquire about a patient's condition she will tell you in so far as she is permitted to. She cannot give you a diagnosis because that is against the rules, although she may in some instances, for she thinks of you as a professional person. When calling in a hospital the clergyman should inquire of the nurse concerning the patient. If you stumble over a bed pan going in to see a parishioner neither your patient's spiritual condition nor your own will be helped by your call. The nurse can help you avoid such an error. If there is a "No Visitor" sign upon the door of your parishioner's room be certain to speak to the nurse, and introduce yourself as the patient's clergyman. In most instances you will be admitted, except at those times when you should not be. If there is still some question in your mind, then call the physician. The nurse works under his direction and is not responsible for the orders he has given except in carrying them out.

The public health nurse carries on a different type of work from that of the institutional or private duty nurse. She is apt to know more about the social condition of a community, the cesspools of crime, and the hovels of poverty than any other person, including social workers. If you are interested in how the other half lives your public health nurse will know; she will welcome your interest and will often turn to you for help in given problems if you encourage her to do so. She will also be able to help you by acting as mediator in those difficult cases requiring a subtle approach. The clergyman needs the nurse just as he needs the physician if his work is to be widespread and effective.

C. *The Clergyman and Social Worker*

It is more difficult to describe the clergyman's relationship to the social worker than to the physician because the social work field is more complicated. There are almost as many types of social work as there are religious organizations, and they come into existence for about as much reason as new religious sects spring up. It is said in Boston that if you need social service care for a flea you will find some agency there for such care. The depression and then the war increased this American tendency to form new organizations.

One cannot speak authoritatively in describing the social work field, but in general there are the public or tax supported agencies and the privately supported agencies. The tax supported agencies work in the field of relief, rehabilitation, child care, health and care of the aged; the private agencies work in the field of limited relief, rehabilitation, child care, family welfare, health counseling or psychotherapy, and care of the aged. The private agencies are now coming to be supported by community chests through voluntary contributions. They pioneer fields of social need and can set standards more readily than can the tax supported agencies. We expect to see a dropping off of private and an increase of tax supported agencies in the future, just as we have seen the church slowly moving out of such social work as the giving of relief, child care and the maintenance of homes for the aged.

We see the social worker, under the term of case-worker, doing pastoral work but calling it something else. The clergyman has not known whether to welcome her as a co-worker or to oppose her as an intruder; actually we find him doing both but unable to understand why he does either. The case-worker has been at a loss to understand the clergyman's attitude toward her because she does not know she is doing a type of work which the clergyman has carried single-handed for centuries. Many ministers have gone into the field of social work themselves and have become leaders there; some have returned to the ministry, for in social work they missed the comfort of the altar. Now we are recognizing that the case-worker has definitely entered the pastoral care field even though she speaks a different vocabulary and her purpose is often different from ours.

When she talks about adequate food, clothing, and shelter for her clients we understand her and join forces with her in trying to coerce indifferent politicians into fulfilling their obligations even though few of her clients may be actually our parishioners. When she takes over the task of caring for orphans and placing them in desirable homes we rejoice and gladly send her families that are anxious to adopt babies. When she is able to counsel with "problem" parents about "problem" children we welcome her help; if she would do something with our neurotic women as we send them to her we would ordain her into full membership in the ministry.

The social worker is content with treating symptoms, as the doctor often is; she talks of "adjustment" which means lack of conflict or suffering. She discovers the clergyman working to establish conflict and blames him for many of the pathological guilt feelings she sees in her people. She does not recognize that the clergyman is as anxious to relieve such guilt as she is and often can do it more effectively, for he has *a different authority*. In time the case-worker will discover, as the physician is just beginning to discover, that the "adjusted" person, like the "healthy" person, is one who has reached a reconciliation between himself and his universe; he is one who has come to an understanding of God and has learned how to live creatively in a world which at its heart is creative.

We should welcome the social worker into the pastoral work field; there is more than enough work for all. Our great need is not for fewer workers but for better cooperation between those that we have, as well as for constantly more able workers, but that is the need in every field. Fifty per cent of our population has no active church affiliation, and half of those who do belong to a church are not in touch with it, while a significant group of the remaining twenty-five per cent do not have a clergyman that can help them in case of need, or they are unwilling to turn to him, for a variety of reasons. As an estimate, the church is serving spiritually perhaps fifteen per cent of our people. What about the rest? Where will they find spiritual advisers? Social case-workers, like physicians, will serve some of them. The others will limp along as sick people do, frustrated and emotionally unhappy individuals, social cancers in the body politic.

Some years ago in Chicago we desired to study this problem of cooperation between the clergyman and the social worker; we decided to do it upon the basis of what had already been done in individual cases. We requested the leading case-work agencies to submit records for the study. In all the records of the agencies we found but one instance where the clergyman had been active in cooperating with a case-worker and that was a bizarre case of a prostitute who kept trying to commit suicide. Our study was not fruitful except in showing us how little cooperation there was.

As a pastor I have turned to social workers for the following assistance:

1. Help in securing positions, particularly for psychoneurotic men, where interpretation was needed with the prospective employer; with a man who had been in prison and who was having difficulty securing work; with a widow whose father was a difficult problem;
2. Persons needing financial relief;
3. Couples who were seeking babies for adoption;
4. Persons needing old age assistance;

5. Persons needing hospitalization who could not pay;

6. Persons who needed the public health nurse;

7. Persons who needed practical nurses;

8. For help in getting patients admitted to a mental hospital;

9. For help with handicapped children who needed to be placed in a home for the handicapped;

10. For help in making plans and securing care for expectant unmarried mothers;

11. For help with a young woman who was having marital difficulty with whom I was too closely tied emotionally to be able to see her problem objectively;

12. For help with a girl who was having trouble with her father and who was blocked emotionally so that she could not talk with a man about her attitude toward men due to her fear of her father.

Only in the two latter instances did I withdraw from the situation.

Social workers have sought my assistance with the following problems:

1. Ministry to the seriously ill and dying;

2. Consultations to decide if a person soon to die should be told he is facing death;

3. Persons facing long convalescence;

4. For help in securing funds for burial of a person who had died;

5. For help with bereaved persons;

6. For help in securing medical treatment for children where no public funds were available;

7. Persons needing marital counseling;

8. For help with aged persons who had few callers;

9. To perform the marriage ceremony for an unmarried pregnant girl and her fiancé;

10. For help in taking patients to mental hospitals;

11. When the husband of a patient died suddenly I was asked to tell her;

12. For help in talking to a boy about going to school who had spent all his life with women and who disliked women.

The clergyman is seldom thought of as being a resource person by the social worker, just as the clergyman often overlooks social resources which the social worker will have or know about. In many larger cities liaison persons, usually clergymen with social work training, are employed to bridge the gap between these two professions. The number of cities employing such persons is increasing.

I used to tell my theological students, "When you go to a community get to know your social workers." One wrote back after a few months and said, "You told us to get to know our social workers. I did when I came to this town. I have just married her." That is one way of getting acquainted across the professional lines, but it seems like carrying the matter of cooperation a little far if the two groups are to keep their individual identity.

XIV

THE LAY PASTORAL WORKER

ONE OF THE GREATEST DIFFICULTIES THE MINISTER FACES IN fulfilling his pastoral responsibilities, as well as in taking advantage of the opportunities, is in having sufficient energy and time for the task. We have seen that there are no short cuts; pastoral work takes time, and it takes energy. The task grows steadily, year by year, as more emotional problems arise and as our people discover the pastor is someone who can help them. Increasingly our clergy will spend their time doing a formal type of pastoral counseling, in the office, by regular appointment. What then about the age-old task of calling upon the sick, the dying, the bereaved, the aged and shut-ins, promotional calling, routine calling, evangelistic calling? There is but one answer: *the layman.*

It is neither possible nor desirable that the church should expect to have a staff of professional workers adequate to do the total task of pastoral care in a church. The staff must be adequate to furnish leadership and handle the more difficult pastoral responsibilities but laymen can be used far more than we have used them in the past. To be sure, some Sunday classes and church organizations have designated members who regularly call upon the sick members of the class, but this calling has been slipshod and often does more harm than good. While such calling accomplishes something when it is well done, pastoral work by the layman must go much farther if it is to make a real contribution to the spiritual needs of individuals, either to those being called upon or to those calling, for both benefit.

We have made religion the "business of the minister" increasingly. If laymen can be drawn into the field of pastoral care they will be greatly strengthened spiritually and the results will be far-reaching throughout the life of the church.

A. *Types of Calls the Layman Can Make*

First, we need to have in mind the kind of pastoral calls the layman can make which will be helpful to the parishioner and enjoyable to the caller.

1. *The chronically ill*—that is, persons who are not acutely ill in that they are suffering severe physical pain, but have been ill for several weeks or months. These persons may be suffering from tuberculosis, convalescing from a heart attack, arthritis or any number of organic diseases. Their great problem is rebuilding their morale, and adjusting to whatever restriction of activity their doctors prescribe—plus loneliness.

2. *Persons who are bereaved*—particularly women, who must readjust their lives following the death of a husband, have a hard time accepting the fact and taking up their lives again. They have the tendency to withdraw from all social activity. They should not be pushed but both pastor and layman must be persistent in their efforts to prevent a grief-stricken person from building a wall of self-pity around herself, and living largely in the past. This work calls for tact and may often be carried on well by persons who themselves have gone through a similar experience.

3. *The shut-ins*—those who due to physical handicap are confined to a home, a wheel chair, a bed; whose bodies are weak but whose spirits know no limitations if they are properly stimulated and guided. The layman who has tact, imagination and some initiative can make the difference between spiritual life and death for such a person: the mind need not die because the body is impaired, but it will unless someone comes to the rescue. "I came that ye might have life and have it abun-

dantly," our Lord said. Through visiting, through good cheer and friendliness that blossoms into genuine affection, through ideas, books, handicraft, and mutual interests, a shut-in's spirit may be prevented from atrophying, and helped to great courage. A gifted layman who follows one or two or three such persons can be of far more permanent help spiritually than the pastor for many obvious reasons. The pastor goes on to another church, he has many pastoral and church duties, he has limited skills in handicraft, while a well-selected layman can meet all these needs.

4. *Older people*—the number of older people in our churches is on the increase. As Maves and Cedarleaf have pointed out in their study, *The Church and Older People*, perhaps the greatest problem older people face, beyond economic need, is for creative fellowship. This may be secured through groups of older people associating together and through visiting. While older people should visit with each other, still younger people should also have the privilege of contacts, pastorally, with them for the benefit of both. Older people need the freshness and natural enthusiasm which youth brings; youth needs the maturity and patient faith which older people have. Both need spiritual cross-fertilization.

5. *Evangelistic calling*—can be done by laymen. Some will have a greater skill at this than others. The pastor will call upon persons interested in joining the church, who are called to his attention by laymen, but a tremendous amount of time and energy can be saved if he calls only upon those who are vitally interested. A pastor showed me a list of thirty names of prospective members he planned to call upon during the Easter season; none of them were known to him; all were known to his laymen and all had expressed interest in affiliating with the church. The practice of evangelistic calling by laymen is followed in many churches, but to have *only* evangelistic calling done by the members of that committee seems both short-sighted and undesirable. What profiteth it if a decision is

reached one day and forfeited in the weeks that follow because of neglect? Good seed and good soil both fail if they are not tended.

6. *Routine calling*—that type of call which is made for no other reason than that a given person is a member of the church, can be done by laymen. In the old Church of Scotland the elders used to call upon every member each quarter and give out communion tokens which were presented at next communion service. Each person's spiritual and physical welfare was inquired into by one who was a recognized *spiritual* leader in the congregation. Laymen, selected laymen of course, can make this kind of call, referring special needs to the pastor for follow-up where it is believed more skilled pastoral care is indicated.

7. *Alcoholics*—with excessive drinking upon the increase, and because of the tremendous amount of time necessary to make any permanent impression upon an alcoholic, this type of ministry almost inevitably must be in the hands of laymen: if possible laymen who themselves have been alcoholics.[1]

8. *Juvenile delinquents*—in many churches there will be laymen, either men or women, who are interested in youngsters who are having difficulties and have gotten into trouble with the authorities. These youngsters need close follow-up and more attention than the pastor usually can give. Therefore, a layman should be interested in such youngsters.

9. The pastoral care committee should have one or two persons who have knowledge and ability in securing employment for persons needing work. These should be individuals who have contacts in the community and ability to interpret personality limitations to a prospective employer, for the pastor and the church often come across persons who cannot compete in the regular labor market for many reasons: physical handicap, past emotional illness and even prison records.

[1] See *The Pastor*, "Counseling with Alcoholics," Forester, May, 1948.

B. *Personnel of the Pastoral Care Committee*

Selecting of the persons who will make up the pastoral care committee is probably the most important single step in the success or failure of this work. Individuals must be selected, rather than being permitted to volunteer. Three considerations should be kept in mind in their selection:

1. Choose individuals who are emotionally disciplined and spiritually poised. The "nervous" person will not do well in this work. There is no objective test for emotional maturity, but after several conversations with a person the pastor should be able to judge him reasonably well in this respect. Some help can be gained through talking with friends of the prospective worker. In fact, the pastor probably should consult with someone whose judgment he trusts in the selection of this committee. Once the committee is working and has an understanding of what makes such work helpful, the members may suggest others.

2. Choose individuals who have some leisure time. We know that the busiest people are the ones who get things done as a general rule, but the busiest one is not always most effective in this kind of work, for unless he has considerable time and energy left from his other efforts he will not be helpful here. Pastoral work requires time, time, time, as must be said over and over again.

3. Choose individuals who like people and who are genuinely friendly. Some will want to serve upon this committee because of their own loneliness. They need to have pastoral care rather than trying to give it. These persons should be drawn into other types of work rather than being used upon this committee until they have overcome something of their feelings of isolation—or they should be used only in selected pastoral situations. If some persist in trying to gain membership upon this committee a discussion with the pastor may help them to understand their desires.

4. The committee should be made up of individuals drawn from various parts of the church's life: men and women, older and young people, members and non-members of the official board, business and professional people, specialists and non-specialists; some who have one interest and some another. Over and above the committee there may be some you call upon for a given problem and at given times to assist in securing employment, for instance, or in a given case of grief, or illness. The committee should have a generous sprinkling of members of the official board, even though they do little other than meet with the committee, for the sake of the church and for purposes of selling pastoral care to the board. Too many of our board members feel they belong to a successful church when its bills are paid and there is a surplus in the bank. While paying bills is important, the *care of souls* is the real business of the church. A well-known preacher, referring to the work of one of his assistants, whose field was pastoral care, said, "It's a good work but it does not pay its way financially." This man needs a first-class religious experience in the old-fashioned Methodist sense.

C. *Training the Committee*

Along with the selection of the members goes the training of the committee before and after they have started their work. This training should be both along lines of increasing understanding of the spiritual-emotional needs of individuals and a study of the skills that go into making pastoral care effective. Training is absolutely essential for the success of the committee's work because the average layman has little or no conception of pastoral care and its far-reaching complexities. Anything that governs effective pastoral care for the minister applies to the work of this committee, the same insights, the same skill, the same devotion to the task; the only difference is in the amount of understanding, the degree of skill, and the fact that the minister is more uniquely symbolic of God and

Christ in the mind of the parishioner than is a layman, even though he calls in the name of the church.

In launching such a program I would plan a four-session course as follows:

1. The first session to be given to describing the task of pastoral care and the proposed work of this committee. This should be along inspirational lines; at the same time the practical needs of the people with whom the members will work should be presented, for there is nothing so challenging as specific human need. The general plan of work, both of individual callers and the group meetings of the whole, should be described. The members should know how much time they must give if they are to be really helpful. At the same time one worker will naturally call upon more people than another. The pastor should carefully point out that this is not just another committee, but that its work is expected to reach high levels of devotion and dedication; after all, what is more important than serving the *spiritual* needs of people? No one is urged to participate but the opportunity is offered to share with the pastor, because of his limited time and energy, in the most sacred responsibility he has.

Closely related to the emphasis upon dedication, the confidential nature of this work must be described. The caller must recognize that he is not to talk about the people upon whom he is calling except with the pastor or with other members of the group. We know that some will not be able to keep confidences completely and that some will make mistakes, but a constant emphasis must be placed upon this point. It is better to be too careful than to be careless. It is for this reason that a small group is preferred.

2. Secondly, a discussion of the kind of needs which are faced in pastoral care should be presented. Ultimately this will call for a careful discussion of problems peculiar to all the situations enumerated at the beginning of this chapter, but this

should not be attempted at first lest the group become so weighed down with knowledge that they fail to start work. This discussion should be of a general nature, combining material found in the early part of this chapter, that found in Chapter II, and other material which the pastor will have available from pastoral work books and journals.

3. At another session, there should be a presentation and study of the *Ministry of Listening.* Such a presentation should take a full period of study. In this connection there are three pamphlets available that can be put into the hands of each member of the committee. All may be secured from the Department of Literature of the Federal Council of Churches, *The Ministry of Counseling,* May; *A Counseling Viewpoint,* Rogers; *The Ministry of Listening,* Dicks.

4. The final period should be given to a study of *the relationship* and what it means in pastoral work; how to recognize it and how to establish it. This force must be clearly understood and its importance recognized if pastoral work is to be successful. The leader should emphasize this point strongly and try to make it as clear and as significant as possible, for it is here we see the *Grace of God Itself* at work. If *the relationship* is strong the parishioner will be helped; otherwise the work will fail.

A bibliography for further study is suggested at the end of the chapter. These books should be available to the group and from time to time a presentation of one of them can be made by a member of the group, and followed by discussion. Also verbatim reports of work with a given person can be studied by the group. This is probably the most fruitful type of study method that is known for the improving of one's skill in pastoral work. If your group is made up of persons of various ages care must be taken to encourage the younger callers to participate in the discussion.

Once the committee has started its work regular meetings of the entire group should be held, twice each month as a minimum and perhaps oftener in a large and active church, depending upon the desires of the members. One church I know of gives a free dinner to the members of its evangelistic committee which meets every week.

At the outset the assignments will be made by the pastor, but as times goes on a committee may handle this detail for him. In some instances a given person will specialize in a certain type of problem; in others several different types may serve better to keep up one's interest. This is similar to a pastor's work for he calls upon and counsels with many different people with many kinds of spiritual needs.

Another way to enlist the assistance of lay pastoral workers is simply to ask a given individual to call regularly upon another and report back to you the success of the call; through multiplying such requests with several selected persons calling is quietly started. As such work develops and as you see who is helpful, selected reading may be put into the callers' hands and their interest stimulated until you are ready for a more formal organization.

If laymen are to be used as pastoral callers, and there seems to be no other way of meeting the tremendous need for more pastoral care, the minister will have to give time to enlisting and training persons who will do it, but the benefits from such efforts will be far-reaching both in the lives of individuals and in the spiritual life of the church. The minister thus becomes, even in his pastoral care, what he has been called in other phases of his work, "a leader of leaders."

Books Recommended for Laymen Interested in Pastoral Care

What Men Live By, Cabot, Houghton-Mifflin
On Being a Real Person, Fosdick, Harper
Interviewing: Its Principles and Methods, Garrett, Family Welfare Society
The Church and Older People, Maves and Cedarleaf
Alcohol Explored, Haggard and Jellinek, Doubleday
The Art of Ministering to the Sick, Cabot and Dicks, Macmillan
Emotional Problems of Living, English and Pearson, Norton

Their Mothers' Sons, Strecker, Lippincott
Understandable Psychiatry, Hinsie, Macmillan
Pastoral Counseling, Hiltner, Abingdon-Cokesbury
Physicians of the Soul, Kemp, Macmillan
Where Do People Take Their Troubles? Steiner, Houghton Mifflin
So You Want to Help People, Wittenberg, Association Press
The Rights of Infants, Ribble, Columbia University Press
Mental Illness: A Guide for the Family, Stern, Commonwealth Fund
Mind and Body, Dunbar, Norton

APPENDIX A

SPECIALIZED PREPARATION FOR
PASTORAL WORK AND COUNSELING

REFERENCES ARE MADE OFTEN TO SPECIAL TRAINING FOR PASTORAL work. Many ministers and theological students feel themselves attracted to the ministry of pastoral care but are at a loss to know what the needs are or how to prepare themselves for such a ministry.

The greatest single need is for persons, both men and women, who will prepare themselves to serve as assistant and associate ministers in large churches, devoting their time to pastoral calling and counseling, with a minimum responsibility in organizational work and preaching. Work of this kind presents some difficulties, but unless the problems of staffing our large churches can be solved the cause of religion will suffer seriously. In some large churches, that is, those with memberships from eight hundred to four and five thousand, the people receive little pastoral care beyond a brief ministry to a few of the sick, the dying and the bereaved. The pastors of the large churches almost universally recognize the seriousness of this situation but are unable to find assistants with adequate preparation for the task. It will be only a short time until training will be available for those desiring to prepare themselves for this ministry.

A second need is for pastors who will prepare themselves for an institutional ministry such as work in hospitals, both mental and general, in homes for children, and homes for older people, and in prisons. While the need is not great the number of institutions that are seeking trained chaplains is steadily increasing, particularly among those that are tax-supported. There has been a flurry of interest among church-affiliated hospitals in the chaplaincy program, but the fact remains that the Protestant churches do not know why they are in the hospital business. It must be remembered that the modern hospital chaplaincy program, both in mental and general hospitals, had its start in non-church institutions: the one in a state mental hospital, the other in a non-sectarian private hospital (Worcester State Hospital and Massachusetts General Hospital). I have worked in both church and non-church hospitals; I cannot see that as a chaplain I had any greater freedom or influence in one than in the other, although theoretically this should not be true. If one can content himself with working in a secondary position of influence and serving the spiritual needs of desperately needy persons while he is constantly irritated by routine, red tape and resistance, the institutional ministry affords a great opportunity.

Administrators of hospitals, homes, and prisons are constantly appointing clergy as their chaplains who have had no specialized preparation for the task. This is neither to the credit of the institutions nor of the clergy who accept such appointments. A minimum of a year's specialized preparation under supervision is needed for work as an institutional chaplain.

A few of our clergy have turned to private counseling as a profession, working upon a fee basis, securing licenses as psychotherapists. The number going into such practice will probably increase in the future in America as it has on the Continent of Europe and in the British Isles. Preparation for this work should also include a period of supervised clinical training in a mental hospital.

As said elsewhere, the two clinical training movements for theological students and clergy started independently of each other in two separate cities in 1925. At present supervised clinical training for clergy is available through several groups. While we hope the time may come when one central office may serve as a clearing house for all recognized clinical training, at present there is no such office. Information may be secured by writing to the Secretary of the Department of Pastoral Services, Federal Council of Churches of Christ in America, 297 Fourth Avenue, New York, 11, New York; also, to the Council for Clinical Training, Inc., 2 East 103rd Street, New York, 29, New York; The Institute for Pastoral Care, Harvard Divinity School, Cambridge, Mass.; Andover-Newton Theological School, Newton Centre, Mass.; or to me at the Divinity School of Duke University, Durham, North Carolina.

For an interpretation and description of clinical training see *Clinical Pastoral Training*, edited by Seward Hiltner and published by the Federal Council of Churches of Christ in America. While there are differences of opinion among leaders in the field, in general, we agree that clinical training for theological students and clergy consists of: (1) work with individuals; (2) the work must be done under the supervision of an experienced pastor and teacher; (3) written records must be kept of the work. Whether the work is done in a mental or general hospital, in a prison, social service agency, or in a local church is of secondary importance; although we would agree that the student should have extensive contact with the teachings of psychiatry. We would also agree, I feel certain, that if a pastor is to go into counseling upon a fee basis he should have quite extensive experience in personal work with a competent psychiatrist, usually a psychoanalyst.

The business of the church is the care of souls. Too long we have stood aside and permitted one profession and then another to take over this task.

APPENDIX B

PASTORAL AID BOOKS AND PAMPHLETS [1]

BOOKS AND PAMPHLETS ARE NOT SUBSTITUTES FOR PASTORAL WORK and personal counseling, but placed in the hands of the proper parishioner at the right time they can be great aids to personal ministry. This is especially true when people are facing crisis situations such as illness or bereavement, or when some tragic new factor has entered their lives, as when a relative becomes mentally ill. After the initial pain, there is opportunity for reflection; and reflection may well mean a new open-mindedness. The right reading may be a real "pastoral aid" at such times.

The list given below attempts to be brief without sacrificing major areas in which pastors are called upon for help and counsel. All the materials selected speak more or less directly to some particular need of the reader. They are not, with rare exceptions, abstract discussions, hortatory suggestions, or discussions of social rather than personal problems.

1. For a Philosophy of Life, for Purpose in Living, and for Understanding Oneself.

What Men Live By, Cabot, Boston, Houghton Mifflin, 1914 and later, $2.50. A classic, still useful, leading toward balance and harmony in everyday living, by the late distinguished physician and ethical thinker, especially useful for those in quest of a philosophy of life.

On Being a Real Person, Fosdick, New York, Harper and Bros., 1943, $2.50. Outstanding volume on understanding and helping oneself, to be recommended especially to those with a high school education or above.

[1] Originally published in *The Pastor,* July, 1946, selected by Hiltner and Dicks.

Victorious Suffering, Glover, New York, Abingdon-Cokesbury, 1943, $1. Excellent discussion of the problem of suffering, presenting many points of view for the troubled but thoughtful reader.

Bringing Up Ourselves, Hogue, New York, Charles Scribner's Sons, 1943, $2. An excellent common-sense volume on producing continued psychological and spiritual growth in adult life, by a distinguished social worker. Positive point of view.

2. For Starting, or Making More Meaningful, Daily Prayer and Meditation.

The Meaning of Prayer, Fosdick, New York, Association Press, 1915, $1. Classic on prayer whose value does not diminish.

Abundant Living, Jones, New York, Abingdon-Cokesbury, 1942, $1. Although the worth of this collection of devotional materials varies from section to section, many have found it useful. By the famous missionary to India.

The Temple: A Book of Prayers, Orchard, New York, E. P. Dutton, 1918 and later, $1. A classic book of prayers for general use which has enjoyed a deserved popularity, by a former British Congregationalist, now Roman Catholic.

3. For Prayer and Meditation by the Sick or Troubled.

Thy Health Shall Spring Forth, Dicks, New York, Macmillan, 1945, $1.25. Much the most outstanding short volume of meditations and prayers selected with a knowledge of the special needs of the sick. (S.H. comment)

On Wings of Healing, Doberstein, Muhlenberg Press, 1942, $2. A remarkable collection of prayers and other devotional materials for the sick, but such a large volume that it should be used only with directions.

Meditations for the Sick, Scherzer, New York, Abingdon-Cokesbury, 1945, 25 cents. A sixteen-page pamphlet of well-selected Scripture and prayers, arranged by the able chaplain of the Protestant Deaconess Hospital, Evansville, Indiana.

God and Health, Dicks, Federal Council of Churches, 10 cents.

A description of how God works to keep the body well, written originally by Richard Cabot, M.D.

4. For Those Who Are Tense and Under Strain.

Release from Nervous Tension, Fink, New York, Simon and Schuster, 1943, $2. Popular advice on handling nervous tension, emphasizing physiological rather than psychological aspects. Mostly sound. By a Los Angeles psychiatrist.

Mastering Your Nerves: How to Relax through Action, Freeman, Harper, 1946, $2. Apart from some of its observations on such questions as alcohol, this is one of the most useful volumes available, designed to aid the reader to understand himself, by a psychologist and a journalist.

You Must Relax, Jacobson, New York, Whittlesey, $1.75. The techniques of physical relaxation, with specific instructions on method.

Be Still and Know, Dicks, Methodist Hospitals and Homes, 740 Rush Street, Chicago 11, 5 cents. A description of the art of mental and spiritual relaxation.

5. For Relatives or Friends of the Mentally Ill.

Psychiatry for the Curious, Preston, New York, Farrar and Rhinehart, 1940, $1.50. Effective popular volume on the nature, background, and types of serious mental illness, by the Maryland Commission of Mental Diseases.

Mental Illness: A Guide for the Family, Stern, New York, Commonwealth Fund, 1942, $1. An excellent guide to practical procedures when mental illness strikes.

6. For Alcoholics or Their Relatives and Friends.

Alcoholics Anonymous, New York, Works Publishing Co., 1939, $3.50. The standard "Bible" of A.A. May be available soon in a new edition.

Alcohol Problems Dissected, Jellinek, Federal Council of Churches, 1945, 15 cents. An excellent brief, factual statement of major things science has discovered about the effects and problems of alcohol, by the Director of the Yale School of Alcohol Studies.

7. For the Bereaved.

For Those Who Mourn, The Forward Movement, Cincinnati 2, Ohio. Conventional but helpful message to the bereaved.

If Bereavement Comes, Holman, Federal Council of Churches, 1945, 5 cents. A brief, realistic statement by a man whose son was killed in the war.

Let Not Your Heart Be Troubled, Morrison, Chicago, Willett and Clark, 1938, 40 cents. Selections of Scripture and poetry for the bereaved.

The Will of God, Weatherhead, New York, Abingdon-Cokesbury, 1945, 75 cents. Excellent and readable, popular discussion of the meaning of the will of God, especially in relation to suffering and death.

The Faith of Man Speaks, Woodbury, New York, Macmillan, 1945, $1.75. Excellent selections from the writings of the ages upon the subject of death. A real contribution to the growing literature of consolation.

8. For Husband-Wife Situations.

a. Pre-Marital Preparation.

A Guide for a Man and Woman Looking Toward Marriage, Burkhart, New York, Hearthside Press, 1943, 50 cents. Designed to be used by pastor in step-by-step discussion with couples he plans to marry.

Harmony in Marriage, Wood, New York, Federal Council of Churches, 1940, 75 cents. Especially designed for use by couples engaged to be married or considering marriage, by the Federal Council's expert on marriage and the home.

b. Sex.

Marriage and Sexual Harmony, Butterfield, Emerson Books, 1938, 50 cents. Excellent short volume on the sex side of marriage by a sociologist who is also a minister.

Sex Problems in Marriage, Crane, Tribune Building, Chicago, 10 cents and stamped return envelope. Excellent brief discussion of the sex side of marriage, in understandable language.

c. Sterility.

To Those Denied a Child, Planned Parenthood Federation of America, 501 Madison Ave., New York, 22, N.Y., 3 cents. Small pamphlet addressed to those who have not been able to have children, indicating that medicine may be able to help them, and including a list of hospitals with special services designed to cure infertility.

d. Budget.

How We Spend Our Money, Stewart, Public Affairs Committee, 1944, 5th edition, 10 cents. Where the family dollar goes. Useful when money questions are involved in marital problems.

e. To Prevent Divorce.

Conserving Marriage and the Family, Groves, New York, Macmillan, 1944, $1.75. Addressed to those considering a divorce, by the nation's pioneer educator in the field of family relations.

9. For Parental Understanding of Children.

Infant and Child in the Culture of Today, Gesell, Arnold L., and Frances G. Ilg, New York, Harper, 1943, $4. Generally recognized as the outstanding volume on care of children during their first five years, by the Director of the Yale Child Development Clinic.

How Life Is Handed On, Bibby, Emerson Books, $2. Simple, excellent description of reproductive process.

Infant Care, Children's Bureau, U.S. Dept. of Labor, 25 cents. A little outdated in its point of view, this is nevertheless invaluable to new mothers.

When Children Ask About Sex, Child Study Association of America, 20 cents. Good discussion for parents.

10. For Guidance in Specific Personal Situations.

a. Cancer.

The Fight on Cancer, Little, Public Affairs Committee, 1945, 3rd edition, 10 cents. Perhaps the best simple, popular description of what is known about cancer.

b. Epilepsy.

Epilepsy: The Ghost Is Out of the Closet, Yahraos, Public Af-

fairs Committee, 1945, 15 cents. Excellent brief statement
of the facts on epilepsy.

c. Heart Diseases.

Diseases of the Heart, American Heart Association, 1790 Broadway, New York, 25 cents. Five brief articles by eminent authorities on the types of heart disease.

d. Tuberculosis.

What You Should Know About Tuberculosis, National Tuberculosis Association, 1943. Good brief statement, available free from local societies.

e. Family Security through Life Insurance.

How to Buy Life Insurance, Stewart, Public Affairs Committee, 1941, 10 cents. Good as a preliminary to working out a plan with a thoughtful life insurance underwriter.

11. For Courage, Understanding, Knowledge in the Face of Physical and Emotional Handicaps.

And Now to Live Again, Barton, New York, Appleton-Century, 1944, $1.75. Inspiring suggestions on making new beginnings by one who had to spend years in her room, following an accident.

I Begin Again, Bretz, New York, McGraw-Hill, 1940, $1.75. Inspiring story of struggle for courage after losing eyesight.

Greet the Man, Wilke, Philadelphia, Christian Education Press, 1945, $1.50. For friends or relatives of the handicapped, realistic and spiritually-oriented discussion of how to aid those injured in the war or otherwise.

INDEX

Aged, 105-109; elderly people, 137; older people, 74, 105, 175; shut-ins, 105ff

Aggressive, 32, 54, 56

Alcoholic, 176; excessive drinking, 3

Alcoholics Anonymous, 135

Andover-Newton Theological School, 184

Behavior, 49, 148, 149; defensive, 48; human, 3, 18

Bereaved, 23, 88-93, 174

Berne, Eric, 4

Boisen, Anton, 11, 12

Books, layman and pastoral care, 181-183; pamphlets, 180; pastoral aid, 186-191; psychiatry, 158; the sick, 93

Bonnell, John S., 45

Burkhart, Roy A., 119

Cabot, Richard C., 11, 12, 36, 37, 51, 149, 164; and God, 37

Cancer, 165

Catholic, 51, 111, 112; absolution, 50, 51

Cedarleaf, Lennart, 105

Chaplain, 183, 184

Christ, 10; Jesus, 30, 114; Lord, 14, 15, 32, 38, 174; as mediator, 10

Church, 22, 23, 114; Episcopal, 112, 141; liturgical, 25, 52; Lutheran, 141; Methodist, 84, 107; of Latter Day Saints, 141; Southern Baptist, 141; Roman Catholic, 111, 112

Clergy, 7, 8, 23, 44, 117; see Pastor; clergyman, 5, 8, 35-39; physician, 161-168; nurse, 166-168; social worker, 168-172; clinically trained, 10; minister, 44, and psychiatry, 148-158; pastor's task, 13, 31; priest, 48

Clinical training, 11, 12, 183; see Council for

Coffin, Henry S., 12, 71, 79, 141, 142

Communion service, 107, 109

Confession, 23, 24, 48; need for, 66ff; made confession, 63, of murder, 64

Counseling, 83; see relationship; counselor, 29, pastoral, 83, 124; marital, 120-124, pre-, 117-119; with youth, 124-130; with adults, 131-137; preparation for, 183-185

Council for Clinical Training, Inc., 11, 184

Death, dying person, 52-67; dying, 75, ministry to, 85-88

Duke University, 184

Evangelism, 109-113; calling, 109, 175

Faith, 20; trust, 35

Fairbanks, Rollin J., 11

Fear, 20-21; apprehension, 17, 20; anxiety, 25; worry, 20

Federal Council of Churches of Christ, 107, 180, 184, 185

Fletcher, Joseph A., 12

Friendliness, 30, 107

Freud, Sigmund, 150

Fundamentalist, 7

Garrett, Annette, 45

God, 8, 9, 13, 30; assistants, 14, 34; Grace of, 29, 110; justice, 88; Mind of, 14, 15, 69; working through nature, 43

Growing process, 13

Guiles, Phillip A., 11, 74

Guilt feelings, 21-24; sense of failure, 21; sense of responsibility, 23